"*Ecstatic Prophecy* caught me off guard. I knew it would be good, as both the life and ministry of Wesley and Stacey Campbell have had an impact on me for many years. But little did I realize that what I thought would be a great book for a unique segment of the Body of Christ would actually become a necessary book for the entire Body of Christ.

"It is with excitement that I recommend this book, and it is with joy that I await its impact on the Church—and ultimately, the nations."

—from the foreword by **Bill Johnson**, pastor, Bethel Church, Redding, CA; author, *When Heaven Invades Earth* and *Face to Face with God*

"For years I have consistently seen Stacey Campbell walk a life in God that is completely open to the present, tangible power of the Holy Spirit, yet profoundly grounded by a fierce love for the proper exegesis and application of the written Word of God and the lessons of Church history. Stacey does not approach this topic as a casual observer of a current fad, but as a disciplined, humble, tenacious servant striving to hear and obey the voice of the living God."

—**Robert Stearns**, executive director, Eagles' Wings, New York/Jerusalem

"Stacey Campbell is not only a dear friend of mine; she is a true friend of God. *Ecstatic Prophecy* is an excellent manual of solid biblical teaching, prophetic testimonies and nuggets from lives modeling a deeper devotion to God and fruitfulness flowing from intimacy with Him. This book will challenge you to be more fully possessed by His glorious presence. My prayer is that the Holy Spirit will completely consume us until we truly walk in the 'greater things' Jesus is calling us to."

—**Heidi Baker**, founding director, Iris Ministries

"With truth that penetrates and experience that reveals, Stacey and Wesley Campbell have given us a modern-day treatise on varieties of prophetic expression. Paul the apostle said there are varieties of manifestations, and the grounded teaching contained in this book amplifies that reality. We have needed this book for a long time, and it will add weight and credibility to the move of God in our day and in the future."

—**James W. and Michal Ann Goll**, Encounters Network and Compassion Acts; authors, *The Seer, The Prophetic Intercessor, Women on the Frontlines* series and many more

"Stacey Campbell's book on ecstatic prophecy is very important. Actually, it goes beyond prophecy to ecstatic experience. From Jonathan Edwards to our own day, there have been great defenders of the ecstatic and great detractors. This book will help us make our way through the fog of the debate and provide some solid ground for approaching this important subject."

—**Daniel Juster**, director, Tikkun International

"*Ecstatic Prophecy* is a powerful read that reveals biblical truth and revelatory insight to everyone who believes that in the last days, the Church will be a prophetic people (see Joel 2:28ff). I highly recommend this book, written by my dear friend and associate Stacey Campbell, who has been used to release the prophetic all over the world."

—**Ché Ahn**, senior pastor, Harvest Rock Church; president and founder, Harvest International Ministry

"I love Stacey Campbell! She is an amazing champion and intimate friend of the Holy Spirit. As a prophet and forerunner, she challenges us to go beyond the ordinary and grasp the extraordinary reality with signs and wonders following. *Ecstatic Prophecy* is a clarion call and timely book from the arsenal of heaven to mobilize God's army into divine destiny. Stacey masterfully gives great insight into sensitive issues and questions surrounding the gift of ecstatic prophecy. With scriptural clarity, historical evidence, revelation from the Holy Spirit and her own prophetic journey into this unknown vista, Stacey dismantles the stigmas attached to ecstatic prophecy. She also demystifies this often misunderstood gift of the Holy Spirit by eloquently balancing the Word of God and the Holy Spirit.

"She has paid the price many times to embrace this gift, often standing alone and being misunderstood and judged, but this has given Stacey the authority to speak into this area and help sort things out for leaders and laity. As the saying goes, 'A man with experience is not at the mercy of a man with only an argument.' As the winds of adversity blow, it has only caused Stacey's roots to grow deeper into the Lord. That is the bottom line of this book: to know and love Jesus and lead others to Him."

—**Jill Austin**, president and founder, Master Potter Ministries; national and international conference speaker; author, *Dancing with Destiny*; www.masterpotter.com

ECSTATIC
PROPHECY

ECSTATIC
PROPHECY

STACEY CAMPBELL
with Wesley Campbell

Chosen
a division of Baker Publishing Group
Grand Rapids, Michigan

© 2008 by Stacey Campbell

Published by Chosen Books
A division of Baker Publishing Group
P. O. Box 6287 Grand Rapids, MI 49516-6287
www.chosenbooks.com

Printed in the United States of America

Library of Congress Cataloging-in-Publication Data
Campbell, Stacey.
  Ecstatic prophecy / Stacey Campbell ; with Wesley Campbell.
      p.   cm.
  Includes bibliographical references and index.
  ISBN 978-0-8007-9449-1 (pbk.)
  1. Private revelations. 2. Ecstasy. 3. Prophecy—Christianity. I. Campbell, Wesley. II. Title.
BV5091.R4C36 2008
234′.13—dc22   2008025525

I dedicate this book to Wesley,
who has been my constant and sometimes
my only encouragement
to continue prophesying ecstatically.
Undoubtedly, without you I would have quit long ago.

I love you, babe.
Stacey

CONTENTS

Part 3 Developing the Inner Life of the Prophet

Part 4 Where Is Ecstatic Prophecy Headed?

Foreword

Ecstatic Prophecy caught me off guard. I knew it would be good, as both the lives and ministry of Wesley and Stacey Campbell have had an impact on me for many years. But little did I realize that what I thought would be a great book for a unique segment of the Body of Christ actually would become a necessary book for the entire Body of Christ.

I was raised in an environment where the prophetic was both healthy and valued. While horror stories abound from the abuses of the prophetic ministry, I have benefited personally from its being in its rightful place. Errors still exist and in some circles are on the rise. But reaction to error only creates an equally dangerous error. It was God who "gave . . . some as prophets," not man (Ephesians 4:11). Sometimes we actually can learn the value of a ministry by seeing how much effort is used by the powers of darkness to distort and defile that ministry. If that is true, then we should have a much higher value for the prophet and the prophetic and become as indignant toward the reaction to error as we are to the error itself.

Stacey's research is so thorough with both biblical and historical support that the reader feels safe approaching a subject that often seems frightening. And herein lies the unusual grace upon this book. While Stacey takes us on a journey that some have even lost their lives over, one feels safe from her sound biblical approach and the unusual gift of wisdom that makes the difficult practical. And while *Ecstatic Prophecy* is safe through divine wisdom, it is also wonderfully dangerous, creating the divine tension necessary for all who desire to pay any price in honoring God with their whole being.

I pray that this book is read by the extremists, who although they may have an actual call of God on their lives, have distorted it through their own independence and lack of value for the other gifts in the Body of Christ. Perhaps God will use *Ecstatic Prophecy* to bring them to repentance—and ultimately to a place where their gift brings the strength and encouragement to the people of God that He intended.

I pray that those who have been hurt by the abuses in the prophetic also will read this book. It would then be reasonable to expect the reaction to error to stop. In the process we will recover the use of this essential gift to ensure both purity and strength in the Body of Christ. And those who are presently the "walking wounded" will no doubt be the first to partake of the refreshing place true ecstatic prophecy has in the Church.

And finally, I pray that those who already have a heart of purity and passion for the prophetic will read this book. *Ecstatic Prophecy* will provide the necessary instruction and insight to go further with honor and effectiveness. For in this book permission is given for us to become all that God intended.

This is an hour when extraordinary courage is needed. Stacey has demonstrated that courage by becoming a forerunner for this generation where untold thousands of prophets are waiting to be released to the nations of the world. She has weathered storms, suffered persecution and rejection and sought the counsel of the Lord from His Word and from other seasoned prophets. She has come out on the other side stronger, purer and more resolved to honor the name of Jesus by walking faithfully before the Lord in her call. It is with excitement that I recommend this book, and it is with joy that I await its impact on the Church . . . and ultimately, the nations.

Bill Johnson
Pastor, Bethel Church, Redding, California
Author, *When Heaven Invades Earth*
and *Face to Face with God*

PREFACE

Before one word of this book is read, I want to address two groups of people.

1. To Pastors and Leaders

I know some of you have picked up this book thinking, *Oh no! Now what else is coming around in the Body of Christ? I do not think I can pastor through one more Gnostic-leaning movement and still survive.* I am married to a pastor/leader and have seen firsthand the damage that unrestrained prophets can cause the Church. Sometimes they even refuse to honor biblical authority structures because they "hear from God." This can wreak havoc! The gain prophecy has brought to the Church often has not been commensurate to the pain. No wonder so many leaders despise prophetic utterances and just throw up their hands in frustration.

The perspective of many leaders is: "Who needs this? It is distracting everyone from doing 'the main and plain' of Scripture. And the prophets themselves are too hard to work with! I do not have the time to deal with their idiosyncrasies.

They always seem to try to attract attention to themselves." One leader said to me, "A certain type of person is looking for an argument that allows him to avoid responsibility for what he does. This person excuses himself by saying, 'The Spirit made me do it.'" A different leader told me, "Some of the things prophetic people purport to experience are just plain crazy. They are clearly unbiblical, but I do not have the time or the desire to walk it through with them."

Unfortunately—and I speak as a prophet—we prophets have earned many of the labels given to us. I have met many prophetic people who are suspicious of biblical authority, often refusing to submit to it. Many do not know God's Word very well because they hardly ever read their Bibles, preferring to do only what God tells them directly. They have all sorts of spiritual reasons for their lack of discipline and lack of scriptural knowledge.

History shows that following the Spirit without knowing the Word almost always leads to error. The Bible is clear on authority issues in every sphere, from church government to family (wives to husbands, children to parents) to society. There is no such thing as following God without submitting to authority in these various realms.

So pastors, let me encourage you. My desire and prayer is for this book to be a tool that will help increase God's people in the unity of the faith, knowledge of the Son of God and maturity (see Ephesians 4:13). If any part of this book leads prophets away from the Body of Christ rather than to it, then I have failed completely to communicate what is in my heart.

2. To Prophets

I believe in a coming global move of God, where He will pour out His Spirit on all flesh (see Joel 2:28). This will happen to countless millions of people. According to Acts 2, prophecy will be the primary manifestation of this outpouring.

Undoubtedly, at least a portion of these people will experience ecstatic varieties of prophecy, just as they did in Acts. This book, therefore, is also for the prophets—those who have had real revelatory experiences but have no one who understands them.

Real revelation changes a person. Holy ecstatic experiences mark a person for life. Passions change. Life callings shift. Daily life is different. You change, but nobody changes with you. You are sensitive to things that most people do not even consider and have a perspective that few others do, and it is difficult to know how to live in the flesh and walk in the Spirit at the same time.

At these times it is helpful to have a confessor, like they do in certain monastic movements. A confessor is a person to whom you can tell your spiritual experiences in an atmosphere of safety and who will help you be rational though revelatory. A confessor helps to keep you doing earthly good when you get too heavenly minded. My husband, Wesley, has been this for me, and his wisdom and counsel have given me the other side of what I have seen "in part." He has a completely different mix of spiritual gifts than I have, and this is awesome. He shows me how he views life but not in a hostile manner. A good confessor is someone who does not agree with you all the time, who challenges you and does not let you stay in self-pity or rejection and who takes the time to hear you when you have not yet found the right words for everything you "know." Having a good confessor has allowed me to see that my piece is only one part of a whole. Because of Wesley's input, I really appreciate the strengths of those in the Body of Christ with other giftings—apostles, pastors, teachers, etc. I know that I need the rest of the Body to bring my small perspective into God's great, big, macro plan for all the billions of people on the earth.

I found the phrase "good confessor" while reading *The Way of Perfection* by Teresa of Avila. She described how much easier it was for her to function when she had a good confessor. But when her confessors did not understand her, she would cave in inside and want to quit. It is helpful for prophets to be able to articulate their myriad thoughts, feelings and impressions in a safe environment. It lowers the interior pressure.

Disclaimer

I also want to add a disclaimer right here at the beginning of the book. I fully realize that the Bible portrays many forms of prophetic expression: dreams, visions, words of knowledge, words of wisdom, prophetic mime, prophetic song, etc. I love all of them, and though this book focuses primarily on one form of expression, I know God communicates through a variety of prophetic forms. The form through which God chooses to speak is not an indication of value. In other words, I do not believe that ecstatic experiences are better than other biblical experiences. The best experiences are the ones that cause God to be worshiped most. These can take any form. It is not my intent, therefore, to promote one form over another. Admittedly, I speak out of my personal experience. Just as other prophets might be experts on dreams and visions and write books about those forms, I am simply communicating what I know best.

In Conclusion

I desire that apostles and prophets work together (see Ephesians 2:20), that prophets and teachers work together (see Acts 13:1; 1 Corinthians 12:28) and that the marriage between the Word and the Spirit is a healthy one. May this book give understanding to those who observe ecstatic prophecy from without, and may it give language to those who experience it from within.

Stacey Campbell

ACKNOWLEDGMENTS

I would like to honor and acknowledge Pastors David and Carleen Kalamen, who have been an incredible source of encouragement to me personally through the writing of this book. I appreciate your friendship and support.

I would also like to thank Tina-Marie Axenty; Deana Van Fleet; Elin Froitland; Barry Keith; Neil, Louise and Grace Livingstone; Dawn Meier; Annette Norman; Timothy and Karen Pond; Joanne Swim—all of the volunteers and staff at Hero Resources and Be A Hero. You keep my whole life in order and without all that you do, my life would surely fall apart.

And my dear children, Caleb, Judah, Joab, Simeon and Vashti . . . "I'll Love You Forever." I still cry when I read that book.

INTRODUCTION

This is eternal life, that they may know You, the only true
God, and Jesus Christ whom You have sent.

John 17:3

This book is ultimately about knowing God. Every true
prophetic experience leads to an increased *knowing* of
God, for by its very nature prophecy is "the testimony
of Jesus" (Revelation 19:10). It points to Him, unveils Him and
testifies of Him. The disclosure of Himself (see John 14:21)
is not something Jesus gives to just anyone (see John 2:24).
On the contrary, revelation of the person of God demands
pursuit. Unlike miracles, which Jesus gives freely and exhorts
us to do (see Matthew 10:8; John 2:23), Jesus' self-disclosure
comes only with desire.

Desire earnestly spiritual gifts, but especially that you may
prophesy.

1 Corinthians 14:1

You will seek Me and find Me when you search for Me with
all your heart.

Jeremiah 29:13

He who has My commandments and keeps them is the one who loves Me; and he who loves Me will be loved by My Father, and I will love him and will disclose Myself to him.

John 14:21

The above Scriptures show that love and desire beget revelation. Even though we all are saved by grace through faith, so that none of us can boast (see Ephesians 2:8–9), and even though we love Him only because He first loved us (see 1 John 4:10, 19), it is possible to pursue God beyond personal salvation into depths of intimacy and understanding. Biblically this is evident both by prescription and description. Among the Twelve, three were set apart. Peter, James and John were allowed to see more of who Jesus was than the rest of the disciples (see Matthew 17:1–9; Luke 8:51–56). But more than anyone else, it was John who was allowed into the most intimate places of Jesus' heart and who seemed to understand at a different level the deeper intentions of Jesus' words and life. As a result, John was singled out, set apart, to receive revelation beyond what the other disciples received (see John 13:22–26; 21:20–22; the entire book of the Revelation of Jesus Christ). Because of this deeper understanding, John's gospel account of Jesus is not as much about His deeds as it is about His nature. "The Word became flesh...and we saw His glory" (John 1:14). John contemplated God in the life of Jesus and "every concrete event of Jesus' life [became an] opening to the divine. . . . There in the 'opening,' each event [told] us something of God's inner life."[1]

I believe that desire is the primary door opener to the things of the Kingdom of God. "But seek first His Kingdom . . . and all these things will be added to you" (Matthew 6:33; see also Matthew 7:7–8). The injunctions "seek," "ask" and "knock" have their roots in desire. I have personally discovered that every "new" revelation of Jesus creates more hunger and more thirst for His presence. Having tasted Him, there is nowhere else to go but deeper into Him. Ecstatic prophecy has been

22

the driving force in my personal journey to know God in the most intimate and eternal sense (see John 17:3). And it is my prayer that this book will instill and inspire desire, earnest desire, for the true Spirit of prophecy—the Spirit that reveals Jesus (see Revelation 19:10).

Stacey Campbell
August 2007

PART 1

ALL ABOUT
ECSTATIC
PROPHECY

1

Inside the World of Ecstatic Prophecy

The room grew quiet as the women prophesied. The man over whom they were prophesying was crying, and his tears were falling on his hands, which were folded across his lap. He definitely needed a Kleenex, but none was available. I was sitting in the corner, listening to the prophecy, intently observing the impact the words were having on the man. I knew him well and had never seen him cry before, but the prophetic words were speaking so directly into the deepest parts of the man's heart that he could not help but weep. This was my first up-close-and-personal observation of the effect of prophecy, and I must admit I was surprised. I had been taught that the biblical gift of prophecy had not only passed away, but also that any type of current prophetic ability could be only demonic. My theology at that time, however, was incomplete, and in the years that have passed since this initial encounter I have seen many grown men cry when the Spirit of God touches the deepest parts of who they are. Back then prophecy was new to me, and my preoccupation at the time was with its external effects. I sat there thinking, *Someone should get the man a Kleenex!* Since I was the farthest from the door, however, I did not want to disturb the sacred moment by getting up and moving around.

As I sat silently staring at the crying man, something began to happen to me. Out of nowhere my foot began to shake. As though it had a will of its own it trembled, softly at first, then forcefully. The shaking moved from my foot up my leg and down my other leg. My stomach instantly filled with a strong wind that began pushing up my windpipe and out of my mouth. My body began to bounce like a jackhammer—up and down off my chair—as my head shook violently from side to side. No one was praying for me or touching me. *What is going on?* I wondered. I did not feel afraid, yet I was unable to comprehend what was happening to my body. I was not initiating this experience at any level. I was being overcome by the Spirit of God, and much like the 120 disciples on the Day of Pentecost (see Acts 2) it was affecting my body in ways that were beyond my control. I was as surprised as anyone when the wind burst out of my mouth, forming into a language I had never spoken before. I found myself speaking in tongues at the top of my lungs.

This was my first encounter with the phenomenon known as *ecstatic prophecy*, or divine spirit possession. What I experienced that night for the first time, which I had never heard of and which I thought was something new, was actually nothing new at all. I would soon discover that forms of ecstatic prophecy have existed since Old Testament times. That night, however, no one was more shocked than I was to experience such phenomena. I was perplexed, amazed and bewildered. I had neither asked for this nor sought it, and I had been taught in Baptist seminary that prophecy—all forms of it—had ceased. I was further taught that any "so-called" supernatural experiences that existed today were emotional at best and demonic at worst. And here I was, shaking, bouncing, speaking in tongues, totally overcome by the Spirit who supposedly did not move this way any more. I recall feeling quite normal and calm inside—not emotional or fearful. Furthermore, I was in a prayer meeting, praying to Jesus who was healing a man's soul. I had no grid for such a thing. But it was the beginning of a whole new world for me, and following the Spirit into this world has taken me deeper into the heart of God.

When Ecstatic Prophecy Occurs

Ecstatic prophecy occurs when a person is completely over-taken by the Holy Spirit—body, soul and spirit—and proph-esies while in this state, usually in oracular fashion. It is, to quote David Aune, a form of "possession trance," meaning that the Holy Spirit comes upon a person, takes over his or her body and speaks through him or her. The physical posses-sion is as real as the spiritual and sometimes occurs against or above the prophet's will (see 1 Samuel 19; Isaiah 6; Daniel 7; John 4; Acts 2). Christian mystics throughout the ages have claimed similar experiences, some wilder than others, and revival history is replete with various forms of visible ecstasy ranging from drunkenness to jerks, to transports, to violent shaking.

My Dream

I knew none of this over twenty years ago when I first expe-rienced the power of the Holy Spirit. I was a product of my religious environment, generally critical about emotionalism and manifestations. Even so, I was a genuine seeker of God. I had searched for God since I was a young child because at six or seven years old I had my first vision of Jesus.

I had been to a daily vacation Bible school in my tiny village in rural Saskatchewan. The Bible school teacher had told the story of the children coming to Jesus, and I vividly remember those flannel-graph pictures of Jesus. *How kind He looks*, I thought in my child's mind. I was strangely drawn to the story and had an overwhelming desire to see Him, to climb onto His lap as those other children did. I was so affected by that story that I prayed before I went to sleep that night, "Jesus, I want to see You. Can I please see You like the other kids saw You?" The Lord answered my prayer that very night in a dream.

As I slept Jesus Himself appeared to me, but He was nothing like the story in the flannel-graph. Instead of His kindness, I felt the terror of His majesty. First of all, He was huge. Immense. Gigantic. He appeared in front of me, and I recognized Him instantly. Remembering how He had let the children come to Him, I began to run in His direction. As I ran, however, He began to speak. His voice was like thunder, booming not only outside but also inside me. I was instantly overcome with dread. I stopped running and fell on my face, covering my head with my hands, as though to protect myself from the raw power of His being. His words were simple: "Christ has died; Christ is risen; *Christ will come again!*" Simple but unforgettable words. The emphasis was distinctly on the final line: "*CHRIST WILL COME AGAIN!*"

The image of Jesus and the echo of that thundering voice have never left me. Though I was young and did not understand it at the time, my whole life would be forever changed from that one encounter. From that moment I knew that God was real, that He was coming again, and innately I understood that He deeply cared that I do good and not evil. Ever since, as though by impartation, I have had a strong understanding of the difference between right and wrong. That one dream birthed in me an acute conscience, which has kept me from much sin and kept me searching for God at every season of my life. I received a gift from seeing Jesus that night: an impartation of the fear of the Lord.

The Fear of the Lord

Many biblical prophets have been gripped with a fear of the Lord at the beginning of their ministries (see Isaiah 6:5; Ezekiel 1:28; Jeremiah 1:6–8; Jonah 1:3). What many do not understand when they read these biblical accounts is that the deeper effect created by "visions of God" (Ezekiel 1:1) is longing. From the dream I had, the imprint of God remained, and after I saw Him that one time all I wanted was more of Him. Now I knew that He was there and that He was not silent.

My problem was that I did not know how to find Him again. I was in an environment where I was not encouraged to read the Bible. Although I continued to pray nightly, it would be many years before I had another dream. Yet I could not get rid of the desire I had to know God. In fact, from the initial impartation that desire is still with me today. It never leaves me, and to this day it compels me to pursue Him . . . no matter what the cost.

The Burning Fire

The Bible and Church history both reveal a pattern of those who see God longing only to see Him again. Moses is my favorite example of this principle. His journey with God began with an audible voice booming out of a burning bush. Oddly enough, the bush burned but did not burn up. This is a picture of what God's appearing does to a person. He who is a Consuming Fire consumes but does not burn up. Other examples of this pattern can be found in the New Testament. When Jesus appeared to the disciples on the road to Emmaus, something happened inside those men: Their hearts began to burn (see Luke 24:32). John the Baptist is described as a burning man—a burning and shining lamp (see John 5:35). These men were touched by God, and like the bush they burned from the inside out but were not consumed. They were on fire with an unquenchable desire to know God.

When Moses first saw the un-consuming Consuming Fire, he literally dropped all to follow Him (see Exodus 4:20). Enviably, Moses saw more of God than any other person in the Old Testament. As a result, he burned but did not burn out. After the burning bush—an extraordinary miracle in and of itself, Moses went on to become the spokesperson for God, the channel for His demonstrations of power. One encounter with the fire of God and he was transformed into the deliverer of a nation. Moses was changed simply by hearing that voice, by seeing that fire. What he heard and saw that day altered his life and consequently the lives of millions of Israelites. He released national judgments. He led an entire generation out of slavery. He lifted his staff and parted rivers, struck rocks and water flowed, was miraculously sustained for forty years with food and clothing that never wore out. He saw not simply a one-day miracle where five thousand were fed, but every day for forty years he saw millions of people nourished only by the power of God! Moses experienced more of God than any other recorded human being. Because he saw, he burned. And because he burned, he always pursued.

More of God

The most striking thing to me about Moses is that one experience of the power of God was not enough for him. His prayers reveal longing. Every taste of God created more thirst for Him. He saw God; he talked with Him "face to face, just as a man speaks to his friend" (Exodus 33:11). Later he even had lunch with God on the sapphire sea (see Exodus 24:9–11). Then he went into the cloud of glory and received the tablets written by the finger of God, and he came out glowing (see Exodus 24:12–18). Still he longed for more. The prayers at the end of his life show the depth of his desire: "If I have found favor in Your sight, let me know Your ways that I may know you, so that I may find favor in Your sight" (Exodus 33:13). He loved

God so much that all he wanted to do was please Him. He pressed on to know God—all of Him, not just a part. How many of us would have stopped at the experience of power and not pushed through to pray, "Teach me Your ways"?

Moreover, beyond the ways of God Moses got to see what had been hidden from all other men—His glory. Longing made him ask for something no other man ever saw ("Show me Your glory!" [Exodus 33:18]) until the birth of Christ (see John 1:14). This is the power of revelation, and this is why we must desire prophecy.

Prophecy reveals Jesus, and every revelation of Jesus breeds longing for more of God. Faith pleases God (see Hebrews 11:6), and it is true that whether or not we ever have a dream, vision or any other form of revelation, we can bring great pleasure to the heart of God simply by having faith. Jesus did say, "Blessed are they who did not see, and yet believed" (John 20:29). Nothing, however, creates a thirst for the presence of God like revelation.

Prophecy creates desire for Jesus. When He appears or shows Himself, the heart is pierced, and longing is left in the heart for more of Him. This is why I love prophecy—all forms of it—because it points to Him (see Revelation 19:10), and He is the ultimate object of man's desire. The Spirit of prophecy, the unveiling of Himself, gives us a foretaste of heaven when we will finally see Him face to face. This is why we should "especially desire" prophecy (see 1 Corinthians 14:1).

Poured Out on All Flesh

It is interesting to think that one day the Spirit of God will be poured out on *all* flesh (see Joel 2:28). What will it look like when that happens? What can this mean? Does it mean that all will become believers in Jesus? Or does it mean that the testimony of Jesus will be manifested globally? Perhaps at that moment when Jesus is revealed through the Spirit of prophecy on a global level, suddenly every knee will bow and every tongue confess that Jesus Christ is Lord (see Isaiah 45:23; Romans 14:11). Certainly there is biblical precedent for unwilling men to be overcome by the prophetic Spirit (see Numbers 22:22; 1 Kings 19). The Holy Spirit will come upon all flesh, and as at Pentecost all flesh will prophesy—likely in an ecstatic fashion, just like they did at Pentecost. The recipients will be overcome as Saul, Ezekiel and Isaiah were overcome—and as the early Church, John and many others throughout Church history have been overcome with the Spirit of prophecy. The resultant revelation of Jesus will rock the world, and willingly or unwillingly every tongue will declare His Lordship over all mankind (see Philippians 2:11).

In the Last Days

It is in preparation for this coming global revelation of Jesus that I write this book. It is both intensely personal and universal in its purpose and application. Having walked the long road from unbelief to faith in prophecy, I want to prepare others for what they may expect when a global outpouring of the Spirit of prophecy hits the earth.

"I will pour out My Spirit on all mankind, and your sons and daughters will prophesy . . . dream dreams, and . . . see visions" (Joel 2:28). Most of this will come through possession trance or revelation trance, as God sovereignly moves. Divinely possessed people may look drunk (see Acts 2) or somehow be made to do what they would not otherwise do. It could take the form of uncontrollable physical possession (as in 1 Samuel 19:18–24) or of trembling and falling like dead men (see Revelation 4; Isaiah 6). Or God could do a new thing, like He did when He imparted the gift of tongues. Prior to Pentecost, the gift of tongues was never mentioned. No one in biblical history spoke in tongues before that day. We all may be shocked at what the global outpouring of prophecy will look like. We do know, however, that it will happen to believers and unbelievers alike. We do know that it is coming and that it cannot be stopped. The Word of God is unswervingly clear on this (see Joel 2; Acts 2).

Sometimes when I think about the coming global outpouring of prophecy I am reminded of a time many years ago when my husband, Wesley, and I took a trip to Rome. While there, we went to a rather macabre medieval church called "The Church of the Bones." It was thus named because virtually the entire building was made from the bones of four thousand Capuchin monks. The door handles, the picture frames, the tables—everything in it was designed and manufactured from human skeletons. It is intended to be an eerie reminder of the brevity of life. As you exit the building, a strategically placed human skeleton stares at you with blank eyes, holding a sign—also made with bone—that reads: "What you are now we used to be, what we are now you will be: *momenti mori* (remember you die)."

I feel a little like that when it comes to ecstatic prophecy. I used to look at people who do what I do as being on the fringe, because there was a time when Holy Spirit possession was a foreign concept to me. What you are, I once was. I believe, however, that variations of what I now personally experience in prophecy will one day be a universal phenomenon, and "what I am, you will be." Not that every prophetic encounter has to be or will be of the ecstatic variety, but at least a portion will.

One day soon the Holy Spirit will be poured out on the entire world, and all flesh—willing and unwilling, controlled or uncontrolled—will have a revelation of Jesus, and they will prophesy that revelation. The danger in that hour will be twofold: (1) people who have never seen it before will reject it en masse, without even asking if it is from God, and (2) the powerful phenomena could lead some into error, if Satan simultaneously pours out a "strong delusion." Both ends of the spectrum are equally dangerous. My desire is that this book prepares you in some way to be a willing and discerning participant in the universal plan of God for mankind.

2

THE UNIVERSALITY
OF ECSTATIC PROPHECY

Ecstasy, mysticism, prophecy, oracles, supernatural or paranormal behavior—whatever one labels them, contemporary culture is seeing a marked increase in the thirst to understand and experience such phenomena. These experiences are claimed by Christians and non-Christians alike, and there is a great deal of controversy in certain circles about whether or not such experiences even belong under the category "Christian." Even a simple study of the Bible, however, confirms that prophecy, particularly *ecstatic* prophecy, has been around for thousands of years. In the Bible, Holy Spirit possession resulting in prophetic oracles is common. Yet in the current Christian culture of the West, such behavior is suspect, frowned upon and often considered irrational, emotional or perhaps even demonic.

This is odd because the earliest witnesses of the Church were products of ecstatic, mystic, prophetic experiences. "Christian literature begins with a handful of letters written by a mystic,"[1] who had been violently converted as a result of an ecstatic prophetic encounter (see Acts 9). The very first members of the Church were birthed in ecstatic prophecy (see Acts 2). The final book of the entire Bible records pages and pages of prophecy received while in an ecstatic state. In fact, much of the Bible—both Old and New Testaments—attests to the regular occurrence of ecstatic prophecy.

And ecstatic prophecy is not limited to Christianity. It is indeed a universal phenomenon. In this chapter we will look at what ecstatic prophecy is and how it has affected people throughout time, crossing cultural, geographical and religious boundaries.

Biblical Ecstatic Prophecy Defined

So what exactly is ecstatic prophecy? The New Testament Greek word *ekstasis* comes from two words: *ek*, "out of," and *stasis*, "a standing." Literally it translates "a standing out," or more colloquially it means being "beside oneself." Ecstasy is synonymous with the concept of religious enthusiasm—where *Theos*, "God," comes "in"—*entheos*. So quite simply, ecstatic prophecy implies that genre of prophecy that is received and delivered while in an altered state of consciousness, or prophecy delivered when a person is possessed by a spirit.

Do not be shocked at that statement. The Bible records that spirit possession can have two sources—divine (the Holy Spirit) and demonic (evil spirits). Spirit possession was not a novel concept for those in biblical times; it was a normal part of the cultural worldview. In fact, spirit possession was somewhat common in that day, as it is in ours.

When we examine (in the next chapter) the Old and New Testament cultural contexts, we will discover that the biblical prophets would have experienced ecstatic prophecy— prophecy received under the influence of, or while the prophet was possessed by, the Holy Spirit (*entheos*). As we do this we will discover just how far the modern Church has drifted from the ways in which both the Israelites and the original Church viewed ecstasy in prophecy.

Words mean what they mean, and when the experts try to find the meaning of a biblical word, they appeal to lexicons, dictionaries, encyclopedias and the like to uncover their exact meanings. Why? Because over time words change. They take on new shape according to our changing experiences, cultures and biases. As time goes on, often a different meaning emerges than what was originally understood by the same word. Take, for example, the modern word *gay*. Not so long ago this word meant "happy or merry." The word is used in that context in the carols we sing at Christmas time (i.e., "Don we now our gay apparel, falalalalala, la la la"). Today, however, if we were to describe a person as *gay*, no one would think he was "merry." Everyone would understand that the person in question was a homosexual. The evolution of this word has caused it to take on a dramatic new meaning. In like manner, time and cultural adaptations also have affected our understanding of how we perceive what biblical *prophecy* would have looked like.

In Bible days, ecstasy in prophecy was pervasive. The more I study this topic, the more I realize how different our contemporary understanding of prophecy is compared to how those in the Bible would have understood it.

Universality

Not only was ecstatic prophecy evident in the oldest stages of the Bible, but it also occurred in many civilizations and many different eras of biblical history and beyond. In fact, ecstatic prophecy is virtually universal in its scope. All religions have their prophets, and all the main religions—Buddhism, Hinduism, Islam, animism, Judaism, Christianity—have ecstatic prophets. I could cite countless examples in virtually every religion where ecstatic prophecy has been experienced.

The phenomenon of ecstatic prophecy was so well known in Plato's day, for example (427–348 B.C.), that Plato gave detailed descriptions in his writings of what it looked like in ancient Greece. It is important to note that long before the New Testament era the Greeks were "familiar with men and women who were endowed with the gift of divine inspiration . . . The Pythia in Delphi as well as the Sibyls are described as divinely inspired persons or ecstatics. Their task was to impart, in an ecstatic state of mind, divine messages or oracles."[2]

Philo, a Hellenistic Jewish philosopher (20 B.C.–50 A.D.) born in Egypt, described the Old Testament prophets as *ecstatics*. Philo's works were enthusiastically embraced by the early Christians and were influential in early Christian thought.

> In speaking of the Old Testament prophets, Philo uses words and expressions directly taken from Greek thought. A *prophet* is, according to Philo, *a man possessed by God*; he preaches words inspired by God; he says nothing of his own, but, *being seized by God and being in an ecstatic state of mind*, he does not himself comprehend what he says. All the words that he utters proceed from him as if another were prompting him. . . . A *prophet . . . is enraptured and in an ecstasy*; his own reasoning has departed and has quitted the citadel of his soul, while the divine Spirit has entered in and taken up its abode there, playing the instrument of his voice in order to make clear and manifest the prophecies that the prophet is delivering.
> Philo's description of a true prophet is exceptionally clear and acute and might very well be taken as a characterization of the prophetic type in the world of religion as a whole.[3]

Ecstasy is not confined only to early civilizations. If one were to travel to another country, another era (over 1500 years later than the culture cited above) and another religion, he or she would find ecstatic prophecy to be alive and well. Within the Sufi sect of Islam, founded in 1273 in Konya (present-day Turkey), the whirling dervishes are totally dedicated to producing ecstasy via dance. These Muslims purposely try to induce ecstasy and trancelike states through a stringently choreographed dance and accompanying music. In the dance-induced ecstasy of these "whirling dervishes," prophetic utterance is said to spring forth.

According to its own legends, the Mevlevi order of dervishes was founded in the thirteenth century by Mevlana Jalalu'ddin Rumi, who whirled in grief after the murder of Shamsi Tabriz, the man who had brought about his spiritual metamorphosis. As he whirled he became "God-conscious." Since that time dervishes have whirled to alter their state of consciousness so that they might receive direct knowledge of the eternal.[4]

Adherents of this Sufi sect claim:

The whirling of the dervishes is an act of love and a dramatization of faith that possesses a highly structured form, in which gentle turns become increasingly dynamic. Chanting of poetry, rhythmic rotation and music create a *synaesthesia* that induces in many a feeling of soaring, ecstatic, mystical flight.[5]

The choreographed pattern of the dance and the progression of accompanying music from simple to complex chord patterns are purposefully designed to produce a state of trance in order to induce prophetic visions or auditions. Adherents also claim that the feelings of ecstasy are real, and as a result it boasts many contemporary North American converts.

Similar to the whirling dervishes of the thirteenth century, animistic cultures of both ancient and modern times use dance to produce ecstatic states. Many years ago my husband, Wesley, was a missionary in Africa. He did community development, dug wells and preached the Gospel in rural Nigeria. Out in the bush late at night in a tiny Yoruba village, Wesley observed people becoming possessed by spirits and having ecstatic encounters during ritual dances. Similar to the whirling dervishes, although at a much faster pace, the participants danced to the loud beating of drums until, as Wesley watched, they gave themselves over to spirit possession. In language very similar to the biblical descriptions of demon possession, Wesley told me how at a certain pinnacle the dancers would jerk suddenly, their eyes would roll back in their heads and they would crumple in a heap on the ground, jerking uncontrollably.

My first exposure to demonic ecstasy in action was at an outdoor Buddhist festival in Thailand. Before I ever saw Holy Spirit-possessed people, I saw demon-possessed people. I clearly remember the scenario, as it was my first observation of spirit possession.

Wesley and I thought we were going to be missionaries, but we did not know to which country we were called. So we bought "round-the-world" airplane tickets that allowed us to stop in as many countries as we liked and set off to find the nation to which we were called. One of our stops was Phuket, Thailand. We were staying with Plymouth Brethren missionaries, and one day we went with them to the marketplace. It happened to be a Buddhist festival day, and the city square was blocked off so a massive idol could be set up in the center of town. A great crowd had gathered around a roped-off section, so we stopped to see what was going on. What we saw scared me. As we watched, curious passersby would stop at the idol, decide to offer incense and enter the area that contained the Buddha. As they entered the square, at seemingly no initiation of their own, they would be seized suddenly by a spirit. Their eyes would roll back in their heads, and even without being able to see they would be propelled, bouncing and shaking, toward the idol. It seemed that they were compelled—forced—to worship and offer incense at the feet of the idol. It appeared that they had no power to resist. When they deposited their gifts at the feet of the Buddha, they fell down, crumpling into a heap beside the altar. "Catchers" would then drag them away, and others would take their turn. We watched several people offer sacrifices, and the physical manifestations of each one were similar.

I could feel the presence of evil, and I just wanted to get out of there, lest those demons jump on me! At that time I was thoroughly uninitiated in spirit possession of any form. All I knew was that I did not like what I saw and felt, and I wanted no part of it. The experience further entrenched my cessationist doctrinal understanding that if anything supernatural happened, it had to be of demonic origin.

On that same trip I listened to genuinely terrified people tell me stories of spirits in their homes and grown men afraid to turn off the lights at night. A Hindu man in New Delhi even told me that he had seen a resurrection from the dead firsthand. That story was an odd one. Wesley and I were staying with a missionary friend from our Plymouth Brethren church. One day he took us to a marketplace, where we went from shop to shop to tell people about Jesus. The Hindus were friendly and gracious, and most of them genuinely liked to talk about religion (as in Paul's day at the Aeropagus). In one shop the owner invited us to sit down for tea. When we asked him if he believed in God he instantly responded, "Oh yes! I have seen His power." He went on to recount how his Hindu grandmother was resurrected when they were carrying her dead body to her funeral pyre. Apparently in front of his very eyes she suddenly sat straight up and "rose from the dead," having died several hours earlier. She was "alive" just long enough to tell the family where a family treasure was hidden. She then told them how beautiful everything was on the other side. Suddenly she said, "I am going back now," and she died again.

Frankly I was troubled by the man's account as, once again, my theology at the time did not have any grid for such occurrences. I finally concurred that demons were alive and well, deceiving people from believing the truth of the Gospel. So I stayed well away from people who believed in the supernatural, thinking I would be safest that way. I was "weirded out" by a lot of what I heard and saw. I could tell that those recounting the stories genuinely believed them, but I did not know how to reconcile the stories with the Bible. Still, to this day I remember the testimonies.

Lest we get the impression that ecstatic states occur only in countries or times far removed from North America, I would like to say that I have talked to New Agers in Canada who have told me about visions they have received in trance-like states. Just recently I sat on a plane with a woman my age who essentially prophesies in an ecstatic state. I talked with her for hours, and according to her self-descriptions, she definitely moves in classic revelation trance. She told me her body actually goes cold when she moves into that state. She called herself a "spiritual translator" who gives messages from one party to another. The woman, however, did not know Jesus. I spoke with her at length about how Jesus has given me visions and talks to me when I pray for people, and she said something like, "Yes, everybody is interested in spiritual things these days. It is no longer fringe behavior."

When I listen to the real life stories of people (all the while asking the Holy Spirit for a word of knowledge that shows God knows them intimately), I have sometimes been surprised at what people have experienced in their search for God. From what I have heard firsthand, I am convinced that ecstatic states and spirit possession can and do occur in virtually every religion, be it Buddhism, Islam, Old Testament Judaism (see 1 Samuel 19), animism, New Age or Christianity. I believe that Christians must understand this far more than they do now.

The Days of Elijah

Sometimes it seems like Christians are the biggest unbelievers in spiritual power. This is not good news. Spiritual power is everywhere, and the Church is moving increasingly into a time of spiritual warfare. How do I know this? Because the Bible says so! It speaks of a future time when the spirit of Elijah will be poured out—the last days. If the fullness of the spirit of Elijah is coming, then even a cursory examination of Elijah's life will show that it will be a time of great spiritual power and miracles. The greater power of God will be displayed, and the false gods of that day will be confronted again head-on. Elijah fasted, prayed and then challenged the power of Baal in order to demonstrate the supremacy of Yahweh. This is what we should expect when the spirit of Elijah comes again in fullness.

To deny ecstatic prophecy is to deny a reality experienced by many people around the world. It is real, and it happens. And in the last days God will pour out His Spirit on all flesh, and they all will prophesy. The Church, therefore, must be ready for this day and understand the difference between Holy Spirit possession, fleshly imitation and demon possession. If we do not understand the difference, then the Church of our day could falsely attribute the power of the Holy Spirit to the power of the devil—just like the Pharisees did when they accused Jesus Himself of using demonic power to perform miracles. At the opposite extreme, if we do not know how to discern between demon and Holy Spirit possession, then masses of people could be led into deception through displays of power. Jesus warned that this was a danger, even for the elect. Both ends of the spectrum are equally dangerous. We must be aware of false prophets, and we must not sin against the Holy Spirit. Only by being intimately acquainted with the ways of God will we be able to discern the difference when the extraordinary days of supernatural spiritual power come upon us.

3

ECSTATIC PROPHECY IS BIBLICAL

The main focus of this book, of course, is biblical ecstasy. Does God allow for it? Does He do it? Does He ever encourage it? Is it something that will die out or heat up in the last days? Since I believe that the latter will be the case, it is important to study the Bible carefully to see what it has to say about ecstatic prophecy.

What God's Word Really Means

The Bible is the standard for all things Christian. We only want the truth, because Jesus is the Truth. No one wants to be deceived, and no one wants a counterfeit. So how do we tell the real from the false? When it comes to money, bankers tell us that the only way to ascertain whether money is counterfeit or not is to become thoroughly acquainted with the real thing. The same principle applies to prophecy and manifestations. As demonstrated in previous chapters, most cultures "believe in the possibility of spirit possession, [and] if the spirits are not considered divine, then they are morally neutral. In the Judeo-Christian tradition, on the other hand, the latter is a theological impossibility. If the spirits are not God's and good, then they must be evil."[1] Therefore, the better we know the Bible, the more we will be able to discern the true prophets from the false ones, the good from the evil.

This is a critical point. If we do not understand the events of the Bible as they would have been understood in their day, then we can misconstrue what God's Word means in our day.

I remember learning this lesson in my New Testament exegesis course in the Baptist seminary I attended. At the time I disliked that class. I found it to be the most "faith deadening" class I ever took. Why? Because the teacher painstakingly took us through every book, examined the historical context, explained the nuances of the text from the perspective of being a Jew in a Roman culture, ad nauseum, ad infinitum. I felt this class would be the ruin of my faith.

Prior to taking the class I used to read my Bible devotionally. "God, what do You want to say to me today? Speak to me, Lord!" After that class, however, all I could think about was what the Bible meant two thousand years ago. I was becoming "sounder and sounder" in my doctrine, but God began to feel farther and farther away. It was not until I had an ecstatic experience of my own that "I got my Bible back," and it became alive to me again.

Yet the older I get the more I appreciate that boring New Testament exegesis class. Though it was hard at the time, I learned lessons then that are invaluable to me now. I learned that we can build our doctrinal understanding only by taking the Bible in context according to the intent of the author. The most accurate doctrine is formed out of what the words meant in the original language in the original cultural context. This does not mean that God does not speak to us without such an understanding, but our doctrinal foundations have to be built from this foundation or else we are in a subjective morass.[2] I learned how to study what the Bible means by what it says, and today when I teach prophets, I highly encourage them to research the historical contexts in order to see the original praxis and intention of biblical truth. When we understand what was happening *then* (in historical context of the Bible), we can more properly weigh and test what is happening *now*.

Seeking Out the Original Meanings

Manifestations of any type generally become a catalyst for controversy. Jesus, for example, manifested healing of a mute man, and the Pharisees accused Him of doing miracles by the power of Beelzebub (see Matthew 12:24; Luke 11:15). Visible and unusual situations often get labeled, but the labels may not correctly describe the substance. When studying the biblical basis for prophetic manifestations, then, it is vital to search diligently for the original meanings of the words used to describe them.

From the beginning God has used prophets to make Himself known to man. He gave them revelation about Himself, and they communicated what they heard and saw. The New Testament affirms this: "No prophecy of Scripture is a matter of one's own interpretation, for no prophecy was ever made by an act of human will, but men moved by the Holy Spirit spoke from God" (2 Peter 1:20–21). All Scripture—the whole Bible— comes from men who were "moved by the Holy Spirit."

There is reason to believe that the word *moved* implies that the prophets were prophesying while in ecstatic states. This word *moved* could actually connote a physical reaction (trembling or shaking) to God's presence. A case for this may be found in the work of creationist Henry M. Morris. In his scientific commentary on the book of Genesis, he made an interesting discovery concerning the first earthly work of God, based on Genesis 1:2:

> "Now the Earth was formless and empty, darkness was over the surface of the deep, and the Spirit of God was hovering

over ['moved upon,' KJV] the waters" (Genesis 1:2). This activity of the Holy Spirit is called "moving" in the presence of the waters. The word *moved* (*rachaph* in Hebrew) occurs only three times in the Old Testament, the other two being translated "shake" (Jeremiah 23:9) and "fluttereth" (Deuteronomy 32:11), respectively. Some commentators relate the word particularly to the hovering of a mother hen over her chicks. In any case, the idea seems to be mainly that of a rapid back and forth motion.

In modern scientific terminology, the best translation would probably be "vibrated." If the universe is energized, then there must be an Energizer. If it is to be set in motion, then there must be a Prime Mover.

It is significant that the transmission of energy in the operations of the cosmos is in the form of waves—sound waves and so forth. In fact, except for the nuclear forces, which are involved in the structure of matter itself, there are only two fundamental types of forces that operate on matter: the gravitational forces and the forces of the electromagnetic spectrum. All are associated with fields of activity and with transmission by wave motion.

Waves are typically rapid back and forth movements, and they are normally produced by the vibratory motion of a wave generator of some kind. Energy cannot create itself. It is most appropriate that the first impartation of energy to the universe is described as the "vibrating" movement of the Spirit of God Himself.

There is another moving of the Spirit of God mentioned in the Bible. "For the prophecy came not in old time by the will of man: but holy men of God spake as they were moved by the Holy Ghost" (2 Peter 1:21, KJV). Here the word *moved* is the Greek *phero*, which in fact is used in the Septuagint as the translation of *moved* in Genesis 1:2. As the Holy Spirit energized the primeval universe, to bring form and life to God's creation, so He later empowered God's prophets, to bring beauty and spiritual life to His new Church through the energizing Word which they inscripturated.[3]

Whether the word *moved* (Hebrew *rachaph*) can actually be interpreted as "vibrated" or not is not the point. Rather it is the understanding of how energy is transmitted and released that pertains to our discussion. Shaking, or vibrating, may simply be a response to power. So the closer God gets to humankind, the more reactions to His presence we might expect. We see throughout Scripture that the prophets are physically overcome, emotionally overcome and spiritually overcome. In the days of the prophets, such overpowering by the presence of God was common.

Nuances of the Words *Prophet* and *Prophesy*

Since I was a French and German teacher by profession, I learned that different words carry nuances of meaning that are not easily translatable into other languages. Sometimes the host language has no equivalent, so it takes a multiplicity of words and a clear understanding of the context to translate the word properly. Sometimes a single word may not do the job.

With that in mind, as I began to write this book I looked back at the earliest parts of the Bible to discover the etymology of the words *prophet* and *prophesy*. I knew it was vital to our modern understanding of ecstatic prophecy to understand first how these two words would have been understood in the beginning stages of prophetic development. I discovered that the oldest form of biblical prophecy finds its root in the Hebrew word *nabi*, which we translate into English as the verb "to prophesy." I specifically wanted to find out two things:

1. What clues emerge from the Hebrew word *nabi* ("prophesy") that would help us understand how the Old Testament prophets received revelation in their cultural context of ancient Israel?

2. Growing out of that foundation, how did New Testament prophets view prophecy?

I felt that answering these two questions would reveal whether or not our twentieth-century understanding of prophecy has changed from how the Old and New Testament saints would have understood it. Is it possible that time and cultural biases have changed our perceptions of biblical prophecy?

In my study I will reference several scholars, but first I want to introduce two of the best minds on the historical contexts of the Old and New Testament prophets, respectively: J. Lindblom[4] and David Aune[5] (please see notes). The understanding gleaned from the life works of these and other eminent scholars will help us understand what prophecy would have looked like to an outside observer in the life and times of the biblical prophets.

I was surprised to discover that most scholarly minds believe that the earliest prophets were all ecstatic prophets. In other words, the earliest forms of *nabi* included ecstatic, physical manifestations. Theodore H. Robinson, past professor of Semitic languages, University College, Cardiff,[6] says that "the Hebrew word for *ecstatic* is *nabi*, plural *n'bi'im* (E.V. 'prophet'), and the verb used of ecstatic behaviour is a reflexive form of the root from which the noun *nabi'* comes."[7] The word is applied to Amos, Hosea, Isaiah and Jeremiah.[8]

The term *primitive prophets* is not used here in any derogatory sense but simply to indicate the earliest phase of Old Testament prophecy, as it is known to us from the oldest traditions, preserved in the Books of Samuel and the Kings ... *It is often said that the distinctive feature of the older prophecy is ecstasy.* But ecstasy is also found in the later prophets. If there is a difference (and there is), it is not an absolute difference but consists in the frequency and the character of the ecstasy.[9]

Most theologians agree that the earliest form of biblical prophecy was ecstatic in nature. In fact, it was not until later Old Testament times that the word *nebi'im* ("prophet") also took on the, may I say, "tamer" meaning of "spokesman." Current scholarship concurs that the Hebrew derivatives for the words *prophet(s)* and *prophecy* (*nabi* and *nebi'im*) came to encompass a range of meaning, which eventually included everything from simple inspiration to the fervor of ecstasy. Having the luxury of hindsight, we can now look at the whole of the Bible and see that *nabi* can indicate anything from inspiration to spirit possession. But in the beginning, the possession aspect was most often visibly demonstrated.

The *Theological Wordbook of the Old Testament* defines *nabi* as follows:

> *nābî.* Spokesman, prophet. The derivation of *nābî* is a matter of controversy. The old Gesenius Lexicon (ed. Tregelles), for example, derives this noun from the verb *nāba,* meaning to "bubble up," "boil forth," hence, "to pour forth words, like those who speak with fervor of mind or under divine inspiration, as prophets and poets."[10] . . . For these reasons this group of authors has supposed that to utter revelations from God's Spirit (ecstatic speech) is the function of the *nābî* . . .
>
> The tendency has been away from regarding the active idea of speaking ecstatically as the essential meaning of prophesying: "Rowley . . . demonstrates [Harvard Theological Review, 38:1–38] that the word *nābî,* though of uncertain etymology, cannot be used as an argument for the ecstatic nature of the prophets" (Eissfeldt, "The Prophetic Literature," *The Old Testament and Modern Study,* ed. H. H. Rowley [Oxford Press, 1951], 142).[11]

As you can see, theologians debate the subject of ecstasy in prophecy. It is common knowledge that instances of ecstasy are recorded in ancient records of many cultures and religions. But both Jewish and Christian theologians are divided on the issue of whether or not the biblical prophets received their revelations while in ecstatic states. It is obvious that:

> The prophets were not mere predictors. Their Hebrew name, *nabi*, comes from a root "to boil up as a fountain" (*Gesenius*); hence the *fervor of inspiration* (2 Peter 1:21). Others interpret it as from an Arabic root [meaning] "spokesman" of God, the Holy Ghost supplying him with words; communicated by dreams (Joel 2:28; Job 33:14–17); or visions, the scene being made to pass before their minds (Isaiah 1:1); or *trance, ecstasy* (Numbers 24:4, 16; Ezekiel 1:3; 3:14); not depriving them, however, of free conscious agency (Jeremiah 20:7, 9; 1 Corinthians 14:32).[12]

Finally, according to *The Brown-Driver-Briggs Hebrew and English Lexicon*, which is the definitive lexicon of its type, the Hebrew word for the noun *nabi* ("prophet," "spokesman" or "speaker") or the verb form *naba* ("to prophesy") means:

> in oldest forms, *of religious ecstasy* with or without song and music; later, essentially religious instruction, with occasional predictions.

> Scriptures cited as examples of 1. prophesy under influence of divine spirit: a. *in the ecstatic state*, with song, (1 Samuel 10:11; 19:20) and music (1 Chronicles 25:1, 2, 3) by the word of Yahweh (Amos 2:12; 3:8; 7:12,13; Jonah 3:1; Jeremiah 19:14; 26:18; 32:3; Ezekiel 11:13; especially Ezekiel 12:27; etc.).

> The same word is used "of heathen prophets of Baal *in ecstatic state*" (1 Kings 18:29; Jeremiah 23:13).
> Another word used for a *prophecy*, is *ne-um*, or an "utterance," (which is often translated "say" or "speak"); can be translated "utterance, declaration, revelation of a prophet *in ecstatic state*, in various phrases" (Numbers 24:3, 15; 4:16; 2 Samuel 23:1; Proverbs 30:1; 2 Samuel 23:1; Psalm 36:2). This word can also be used before divine names, i.e. *Yahweh* (Jeremiah 23:1), as an "utterance, declaration of Yahweh" (prophet

citing divine word given through him) (Genesis 22:16; Numbers 14:28; 2 Kings 9:26; 19:33; Isaiah 37:34; etc.).[13]

There is just no getting around it: The ecstatic state is part of a great deal of biblical prophecy, and all the biblical lexicons and theological books reveal that the etymology of the word *nabi* originally indicated an ecstatic dimension to prophecy. The root words reveal the inspiration dimension: "boiling up as a fountain," "uttering" (obviously out of inspiration).

The question is: To what extent did inspiration occur? It is obvious that there are degrees of inspiration, ranging from passive to frenzied reception. How often was the inspiration accompanied with "the fervor of ecstasy"?

Two Old Testament Examples of Ecstasy

Two classic Old Testament examples of fervent ecstasy are found in the life of Saul. Both are worthy of our study.

The first encounter is seen in 1 Samuel 10:1–12 where Samuel, directed by God, anointed Saul as the first king of Israel by pouring the anointing oil upon his head. The heavenly anointing was prophesied to come upon Saul soon thereafter.

> As you approach the town, you will meet a procession of prophets coming down from the high place with lyres, tambourines, flutes and harps being played before them, and they will be prophesying. The Spirit of the LORD will come upon you in power, *and you will prophesy with them; and you will be changed into a different person.* Once these signs are fulfilled, do whatever your hand finds to do, for God is with you.
>
> 1 Samuel 10:5–7, NIV, emphasis mine

Many Bible scholars have not known what to make of this roving, worshiping band of prophets. They seem to have come out of nowhere, and yet the people of their day knew they were a distinct company and that the Spirit of God was in their midst. In fact, the reference to this group of prophets ran for generations (see 1 Samuel 10:11–12; 19:20–24). The question by all the onlookers ("Who is their father?") implies that this gift was generational, and that it had been passed down from father to son (1 Samuel 10:12; see also Amos 7:14). It seems, therefore, that a spiritual prophetic structure had existed for generations. Even in the days of Elijah and Elisha— and beyond—large bands of prophets were still functioning together (see 1 Kings 20:35; 2 Kings 2:1–15; 4:1, 38; 5:22; 6:1; 9:1; Amos 7:14).

The description of the encounter of the Lord coming upon Saul in power, and later in judgment power, leaves no doubt that there was more going on than mere words (see 1 Samuel 19:23–24). "This passage (1 Samuel 19:18–24) may be called the *loci classici* of biblical ecstasy."[14] "When all those who had formerly known him saw him prophesying with the prophets, they asked each other, 'What is this that has happened to the son of Kish?'"(1 Samuel 10:11, NIV).

> The unusual sight of an aristocrat like Saul prophesying was surprising to those who observed it, evoking questions like: "What has happened to the son of Qish?" "Is Saul among *the ecstatics* [nebi'im]?" "Who is *their [the ecstatics']* father?" It is noteworthy here that the people "saw" something unusual in the behavior of Saul.[15]

David Aune agrees: "As we pointed out earlier, the verbs in this here (in 1 Samuel 10:5–6, 10; 19:20–21, 23), *hitnabbe* and *nibba*, usually translated 'prophesy,' should probably be rendered 'rave.'"[16] John White, a well-known evangelical author and speaker, says of this text:

> The passage seems to focus on the awesome power of the Spirit, which causes Saul to do something he has never done before, and this probably astonishes Saul as much as people who observed him. His acquaintances are watching, and their surprise is clearly caused as much by what they saw (10:11) as

by what they heard. It seems likely that the Spirit's power produced discernible (possibly ecstatic) changes in the prophets, changes the people observing Saul were familiar with. The effects of the Spirit's power evidently lasted for some time (10:13).[17]

The second account of biblical ecstasy, which took place years later, leaves no doubt as to the ecstatic nature of seizing by the Spirit of God (see 1 Samuel 19:18–24). Even the scant picture contained in a few verses is graphic. Saul sent a battalion of tough soldiers to capture David. A reasoned guess puts the number at about fifty men. One thing was obvious: They certainly were not willing vessels on their way to a renewal meeting.

> Then Saul sent messengers to take David, but when they saw the company of the prophets prophesying, with Samuel standing and presiding over them, the Spirit of God came upon the messengers of Saul; and they also prophesied. When it was told Saul, he sent other messengers, and they also prophesied. So Saul sent messengers again the third time, and they also prophesied.
>
> 1 Samuel 19:20–21

Our imaginations can picture the Spirit of God leaping from the midst of these prophets and landing on the heads of these tough soldiers, causing them to prophesy in wonderment. It is obvious that this experience happened against their will; they did not have a choice. And this happened three times with the same result! David and Samuel were in the midst of an epicenter of spiritual power and anointing, and when others walked into it they received spiritual blessing.

What was Saul's response?

> He himself left for Ramah . . . And he asked, "Where are Samuel and David?" So Saul went to Naioth at Ramah. But

the Spirit of God came even upon him, and he walked along prophesying until he came to Naioth. He stripped off his robes and also prophesied in Samuel's presence. He lay that way all that day and night.

1 Samuel 19:22–24

The King James Version says he "lay down naked all that day and all that night." Since this is in the same story, it is likely that the action of Saul ripping off his clothes and being stuck like a bug on the ground prophesying for long durations is the same type of involuntary prophesying that happened to the three groups of soldiers.

This was not a penitent Saul. No, this was an unrepentant man who was seized against his will and taken over body, soul and spirit. An ecstatic condition would better suit the context than a willing vessel. It is uncertain if this condition included shaking ecstatic utterances, as was the case in historical revival settings as well as present-day examples. But the possibility cannot be ruled out. Over the course of his life, Saul had entered the spiritual epicenter of the company of the prophets and ended up becoming one of them. God still has the right to initiate what would seem to us to be the most outlandish spiritual experiences. We would do well to remember that God is God, and we are not!

Ecstasy: A Wide Range of Manifestations

The accounts depicting how prophets receive revelation, however, vary greatly. Some prophesy out of simple inspiration, others out of visions and still others out of ecstatic states. Different scholars use different terminology to describe the variations. Lindblom, for example, makes the distinction between *orgiastic* and *passive (lethargic) ecstasy*,[18] whereas Aune uses the terms *possession trance* and *vision trance*.[19] No matter how ecstasy is described, everyone agrees that ecstasy has a range of meaning and is accompanied by a range of manifestations, which are aptly described below:

> When inspiration strongly intensifies, it turns into ecstasy. Ecstasy belongs to the psychical phenomena, the definition of which has varied from time to time. . . . [It] also appear[s] in connection with other more or less violent alterations in the ordinary spiritual life. . . . I prefer to define *ecstasy* as an abnormal state of consciousness in which one is so intensely absorbed by one single idea or one single feeling, or by a group of ideas or feelings, that the normal stream of psychical life is more or less arrested. The bodily senses cease to function; one becomes impervious to impressions from without; consciousness is exalted above the ordinary level of daily experience; unconscious mental impressions and ideas come to the surface in the form of visions and auditions. . . . It must be kept in mind that ecstasy has many degrees. There is an ecstasy which involves a total extinction of the normal consciousness, a complete insensibility and anesthesia. There is also an ecstasy that approximates to a normal fit of absence of mind or intense excitement. This observation is very important for the study of the psychology of the prophets. Inspiration or psychical exaltation is characteristic of all men and women who belong to the prophetic type. But this inspired exaltation has in the prophets a tendency to pass over into a real ecstasy of a more or less intense nature.[20]

Many times in the biblical descriptions of the prophets the phenomena of trembling, or shaking or physical manifestations such as what resembled drunkenness in Acts 2 are observed. When prophets received the word of the Lord, they were "moved"; they either trembled (see Jeremiah 23:9; Habakkuk 3:16), fell like dead (see Revelation 1:17) or were otherwise overcome (see 1 Samuel 19; Acts 2). They were possessed.

In ancient Israel it was widely believed that the Spirit of God caused the revelatory trance. For this reason a prophet could be popularly designated a "man of the Spirit" (see Hosea

9:7). Old Testament prophets also referred to their experience of revelatory trance as "Yahweh's hand" being upon them (see Ezekiel 3:14; 8:1; 33:21–22; Isaiah 8:11; Jeremiah 15:17). These expressions indicate that prophets could experience a revelatory trance in terms of divine possession or control. The revelatory trance could also be experienced in terms of a vision perceived by the prophet (see Amos 1:1; 7:1, 4, 7; 8:1; Hosea 12:10; Isaiah 1:1; 1 Kings 22:19–23).[21]

T. H. Robinson describes the physical phenomena that occur in conjunction with ecstasy:

> It consisted of a fit or attack, which affected the whole body. Sometimes the limbs were stimulated to violent action, and wild leaping and contortions resulted. These might be more or less rhythmical, and the phenomenon would present the appearance of a wild and frantic dance. At other times there was more or less complete constriction of the muscles, and the condition became almost cataleptic. . . . Face and aspect were changed, and to all outward appearance the Ecstatic "became another man."[22]

Obviously all the biblical prophets would have been overcome by God at some level, and the degree of divine possession, or ecstasy, would have been visible to outside observers through the physical manifestations. Of course, by its very nature, all prophecy is inspired. For this reason, the concept of the biblical prophet as "spokesman," as discussed earlier, should be rendered at the very minimum "inspired spokesman."

Translating *Ecstasy*

Far from being confined to the "primitive prophets," ecstasy carries right on through the Old Testament into the New Testament and beyond. In fact, the word *ecstasy* comes from a Greek word, not a Hebrew one. *Ecstasy* is the English transliteration of the word *ékstasis* and is found several times in the Greek New Testament. When it is translated into English, it takes a variety of words to describe it.

> It is translated "amazement" in Acts 3:10. It was said of any displacement, and especially with reference to the mind, of that alteration of the normal condition by which the person is thrown into a state of surprise or fear, or both; or again, in which a person is so transported out of his natural state that he falls into a *trance* (see Acts 10:10; Acts 11:5; Acts 22:17). As to the other meaning, the RV has "amazement" in Mark 5:42 and Luke 5:26, but "astonishment" in Mark 16:8.[23]

Unfortunately for the modern reader, "trance" may give the wrong impression of what actually happened. To translate *ecstasy* as "trance" today carries a far milder connotation than it would have in Bible times. In the 21st century the word *trance* conveys the idea of a gentle Buddhist staring quietly into space while experiencing a sort of vision with his "spiritual eyes." But this is not an accurate depiction of the biblical connotation.

We must look again at the original meaning in the original context before we misinterpret the English translation, which does not necessarily pick up the nuances of the original Greek. A lot of time has passed, and as we demonstrated earlier, words change over time. In 1611 when the King James Version was produced, "trance" was the best single word in the host language to describe the incident. And if you add to this the issue of theology, then the translation problems are significantly compounded. When potentially difficult theological issues are being raised, they can affect how the words are translated.

When the King James translators were translating the word *baptizo* into English, for example, they knew that this Greek word was a common trade word meaning "to immerse" or "to plunge" (i.e., as in cloth into dye, or food into boiling water). The Anglican and Catholic practice of the day, however, was to sprinkle infants. The translators played it safe theologically by lifting the Greek word from its language and anglicizing it, instead of translating it into an English equivalent as they did with every other word. Hence the word came to be understood as a liturgical water ritual instead of full immersion, which the original Greek word actually meant.

As we have discovered, a similar situation occurs with the words *ecstatic* and *prophesy*. When ecstasy is translated "trance" in the KJV in the New Testament, both the contexts and the original Greek word indicate that ecstasy (possession trance and/or vision trance) was part of the first experience. It had a range of meaning, encompassing both the frenzied activity displayed in Samuel's school of the prophets, as well as a more catatonic suspension of natural senses. In New Testament times, therefore, *ékstasis* would have been understood as it was understood in the times of the primitive prophets. Why do I say this? Because the original meaning of *ecstasy* meant "frenzy"—the type of frenzy that produces awe and amazement.

> In *classical Greek*, ékstasis *means "frenzy"*. . . but may include distraction of mind caused by wonder and astonishment or exceptional joy and rapture. Among the results of the healing of the paralytic by Christ, Luke tells us that amazement (*ékstasis*) took hold on all (Luke 5:26). Mark, in describing the effects of the resurrection upon the minds of the women as they fled from the tomb, states that *trembling* and astonishment (*ékstasis*) had come upon them (Mark 16:8). In Matt. 12:23; Mark 2:12; 6:51 the verb *exístemi* [verb form of *eksatsis*] in the mid. sense is used in reference to *the effects upon the multitude* conveyed by the bestowal of the gift of tongues (Acts 2:7, 12), and of the preaching of Paul in the synagogues immediately after his conversion (Acts 9:21).[24]

This was the original meaning. Yet as I have already mentioned, *ecstasy* has many degrees. In *Vine's Expository Dictionary of Old and New Testament Words*, ecstasy is translated as follows: "amaze . . . denotes 'a trance' in Acts 10:10; Acts 11:5; Acts 22:17, *a condition in which ordinary consciousness and the perception of natural circumstances were withheld*, and the soul was susceptible only to the vision imparted by God" (emphasis mine).[25]

Branded by the Fire

It is evident that in the Bible ecstatic prophecy occurred in both the Old and New Testaments. Most of the prophets would have experienced various forms of possession or revelatory trance, although their experiences varied in intensity. Ecstasy was not uncommon in Bible times. It was an accepted part of the spiritual culture of the day.

It is significant to me that the primitive prophets, all the major prophets and the greatest New Testament prophets (John, Peter and Paul) experienced ecstasy when they received revelation. Instead of ecstasy being a stigma, it actually may be an endorsement of greater divine possession. Quite simply, the more He fills us, the better it is. We feel His emotions, are incapacitated by His power and are branded by the fire in His heart.

4

BIBLICAL ECSTASY AND THE CONSCIOUSNESS OF THE PROPHET

If ecstasy exists—and it does exist in many religions—then how do we determine what is holy ecstasy and what is not? As I said before, for every real experience there is a counterfeit one. So what is the difference between the ecstasy of the biblical prophets and the recorded ecstasy of the prophets of other gods?

The Difference between Yahweh's Prophets and Others

Scholars debate this point, and most of the debate centers on the psychological state of the true prophets versus the psychological state of the false prophets. Most scholars concur that the ecstasy of the biblical prophets could involve the loss of bodily control but not the loss of sanity or lucidity.

> Ecstasy, when it does appear in the Hebrew Bible, is to be understood as *strange actions rather than as strange utterances.*

This fact is equally true both at Mari and in early Israel. To cite Heschel again, "The office of a prophet, which consists of setting forth a message in blunt and clear terms rather than in dark oracles and intimations, must have its source in moments of comprehension and understanding." But the importance of comprehension must also be underscored at the moment of delivery, too. While their audiences sometimes ridiculed what they identified as strange behavior, they seldom had trouble understanding what was being said. *Their behavior may have seemed strange, but the messages of the prophets of Yahweh were above all straightforward, unambiguous and totally understandable.*[1]

The retention of clarity of mind was the significant difference between Yahweh's prophets and the prophets of other deities. Although the body might be overcome, the rationality of the prophets remained.

Drunkenness or Union with God?

In the scholarly material associated with the subject of ecstasy in Old Testament prophets[2] the big point of controversy is whether or not ecstasy caused a loss of personal consciousness. Certain scholars assume that personal consciousness is lost when the deity possesses the person. For this reason they argue against ecstasy being part of the experience of Yahweh's prophets. Heschel makes a case that because of the clear association between ecstatic states and "alcoholic orgiasm"[3] the Hebrew prophets could not have been ecstatics. As proof, he cites several prophets denouncing the "drunken stupors" and confusion of the false prophets (see Isaiah 28:7; 19:14; 5:11, 22; Hosea 4:11; Habakkuk 2:5; Proverbs 20:1; Joel 3:3).[4]

This argument would be incredibly convincing if it were not for the fact that the Church was birthed with the phenomena of what appeared to the outsiders to be drunkenness. The early Church experience—among believing Jews—of being overcome by the Spirit to such an extent that they were thought to be drunk obliterates Heschel's argument entirely. On the contrary, the manifestation of spiritual drunkenness of the nascent Jewish church, with the correlating commentary by Peter that this was the outpouring of prophecy that Joel had prophesied, virtually proves that ecstatic prophecy is thoroughly biblical in nature. The visible possession, falsely attributed to drunkenness, is Yahweh's stamp that ecstasy comes from Him—only without an actual intoxicant. God used the common pagan sign of "alcoholic orgiasm" to demonstrate that ecstasy in Yahweh's prophets was justified all along—from the primitive prophets onward. Ecstasy in and of itself is not bad—unless the source of the ecstasy is a god other than Yahweh.

If we think about it, shouldn't Christians long to be possessed by God? Shouldn't we desire union with Him? Is it not a lofty goal to be totally conformed into His image, to be abandoned to and possessed by His Spirit? Proximity and possession, partaking of His divine nature (see 2 Peter 1:4)—most of the great mystics and the greatest Christians of the Church spoke of such things. And when they describe the times in their lives when, through focused pursuit of Jesus, they attained union or possession experiences, most of them were either physically or emotionally overcome, and their ecstatic experiences totally transformed them. They never thought the same way again. They were God's voluntary "bondservants" (Exodus 21:2–6) and served Him from the heart for life.

Losing Consciousness?

So were the biblical prophets actually in ecstasy when they received revelation? I believe from personal experience that they were. Still, the smartest theologians on the planet are divided on this issue.

The conflict centers on the question of whether or not enthusiasm or ecstasy involves the "extinction of the person."[5] When I prophesy, often with physical manifestations, I can tell you I *never* lose sanity or coherence. Though I am bodily overcome, I am not rationally overcome. From the first moment when my body begins to shake as though it has a mind of its own, I am always acutely aware of what is going on. I have never lost consciousness and been unable to remember what transpired. Yet as Lindblom so aptly pointed out, "There are degrees of ecstasy."

Some biblical texts, however, do beg the question: Did Paul lose consciousness, at least of his surroundings, when he said, "whether [I was] in the body I do not know, or out of the body I do not know" (2 Corinthians 12:2)? Did John lose consciousness of his natural surroundings when he was invited to "Come up here" and see the future (Revelation 4:1)?

I know from experience that God comes close by degrees. I have prophesied in ecstatic states where virtually every word I spoke came spontaneously and from without—almost like automatic speech (for lack of a better description). I spoke the words simultaneously as I heard them. The testimony of the Christian Finnish trance preachers is that they had similar experiences. When "possession trance" occurs, often a demonstrable presence of the *kavod* ("heavy weight of the glory") of God fills the entire room. Like Samuel's school of the prophets, like the Upper Room, like what has occurred in almost every revival in recorded history, the Holy Spirit hits a region and everyone is affected by it.

Once I was prophesying at a conference of almost five thousand people.[6] All was calm until the second I opened my mouth to prophesy. As I began to speak, I could hardly keep up with the words that flew rapidly through my mind. But what happened in the congregation was amazing. Within seconds, three-quarters of the audience were overcome by the Holy Spirit at the same time. People who had never experienced physical manifestations began to fall, tremble, shake and shout. Loud cries and screams emanated from the crowd. I was so shocked at the uproar that I stopped prophesying, thinking something had happened in the crowd.[7] Wesley, who was standing beside me, said, "Don't stop; keep going." So I closed my eyes and continued. Spontaneous deliverances occurred. People told me that they had visions or that God spoke to them. Afterward pastors came up to me repenting for cynicism and unbelief because they had entered the conference skeptically, but during the prophecy they were so bodily overcome that they actually were thrown out of chairs and felt the power of God at levels they had never experienced before.

Another time I was in a crowd of only a hundred people or so in a Muslim village in northern Mozambique. We had just shown the *Jesus* film to the village, and I was preaching through translation to the villagers. I was speaking in English, after which an interpreter translated my words into Portuguese, the national language. Finally, a third person translated the Portuguese into the regional language of *Makhua* (a.k.a. *Macua* or *Makua*). At the end of my sermon the Holy Spirit came upon me, and the Lord gave me a prophecy for the village. The moment I began to prophesy, I began shaking violently. Before the interpreters could even translate the prophecy into Portuguese, let alone into the regional tribal language, two demon-possessed people began shrieking and manifesting in the crowd. These villagers could not even understand English! With no one touching them, the power of the Holy Spirit overcame the crowd and exposed those involved in witchcraft, simply because the demons were overcome by the power of the Spirit of God. Like the demoniac in the Book of Acts said, "Jesus I know, and Paul I know; but who are you?" (Acts 19:15, NIV). As this passage illustrates, evil spirits can discern when the Holy Spirit is there. And evil spirits know that God's power is greater than theirs. Those two people received spontaneous deliverances as the other villagers watched. As a result, many people received Jesus into their lives that night.

Everything that comes out of a Holy Spirit-initiated ecstatic encounter involves a heightened awareness of God and the spiritual world. When I am in an ecstatic state, my mind fills with texts of Scripture. I am lucid and coherent. My understanding is never darkened. Spiritual realities become more real than, or as real as, natural realities.

I do not believe, therefore, that prophets lose consciousness in biblical ecstasy. Instead, spiritual truth becomes intensified/ highlighted/heightened, and I can see beyond natural into spiritual issues. I know information I never knew before. Bible verses that I have not read for years, or perhaps never read, pop into my head. Almost invariably, I have to look them up in my concordance to see where they are. I have noted in my reading of Church history that often those in ecstatic states will quote verses or be able to speak in languages unknown to them. This was true even with children, for example, in the Huguenot revival in France (circa 1689).

> From the mouths of those who were little more than babes came texts of Scripture, and discourse in good and intelligible French, such as they never used in their conscious hours. When the trance [ecstatic state] ceased, they declared that they remembered nothing of what had occurred, or of what they had said. In rare cases they retained a general and vague impression, but nothing more. There was no appearance of deceit or collusion, and no indication that in uttering their predictions respecting coming events they had any thought of prudence, or doubt as to the truth of what they had foretold.[8]

The Prophet and Writings of Ancient Greece

It is interesting to note that the New Testament word *prophet* came out of a secular association with the prophets or oracles of ancient Greece. One of the more famous writers on spirit possession was the Greek philosopher Plato.

Plato is one of the earliest and most detailed informants for ecstatic prophecy in ancient Greece. The Septuagint (the Greek translation of the Hebrew Bible) is the transitional document between the Hebrew Old Testament and the Greek New Testament. It is, therefore, important for us in this study to understand what was happening in the cultural context of the Septuagint. As a primary spokesperson for his era, Plato's writings on prophetic behavior are extremely relevant in giving us understanding of the context in which the Septuagint was written.[9]

Plato labeled those in an ecstatic state *prophetes*—hence, our English word *prophet*. Plato wrote at length on the *prophetes* because he was fascinated by them, fully believing in their supernatural origin. In his writings we learn a great deal about "the phenomena of ecstasy and inspired oracular utterance."[10] Plato saw prophetic ecstasy as "the greatest of blessings . . . com[ing] to us through *madness* when it is sent as a gift from the gods" (emphasis mine).[11]

"Madness" is an interesting way to describe ecstatic prophecy, don't you think? Why would he use such a word? There must be something observable that contributes to this description. Interestingly, the Old Testament prophets, in a time and culture far removed from Plato's, used similar language to describe the prophets (*nebi'im*).

> The LORD has appointed you priest in place of Jehoiada to be in charge of the house of the LORD; you should put any *madman who acts like a prophet* into the stocks and neck-irons.
>
> Jeremiah 29:26, NIV, emphasis mine

> The prophet is a *fool*, the inspired man is *demented*.
>
> Hosea 9:7, emphasis mine

> The prophet is considered a *fool*, the inspired man a *maniac*.
>
> Hosea 9:7, NIV, emphasis mine

71

Now Elisha the prophet called one of the sons of the prophets and said to him, "Gird up your loins, and take this flask of oil in your hand and go to Ramoth-gilead. When you arrive there, search out Jehu. . . . Then take the flask of oil and pour it on his head and say, 'Thus says the LORD, "I have anointed you king over Israel."' Then open the door and flee and do not wait." . . . Now Jehu came out to the servants of his master, and one said to him, "Is all well? Why did this *mad fellow* come to you?" And he said to them, "You know very well the man and his talk."

2 Kings 9:1–3, 11, emphasis mine

"Madmen acting like prophets," "fools," "demented by inspiration," "maniacs," "mad fellows"—these are biblical descriptions of prophets by the prophets. And these descriptions of prophets in the Old Testament precede Plato by hundreds of years. Jeremiah, quoted above, lived a full two hundred years before Plato, and hundreds of miles away from Athens, where Plato lived and wrote. And Hosea lived almost 350 years before Plato. It is inconceivable, therefore, that the Bible is borrowing from classical Greek thought when it describes prophetic behavior.

In fact, the Hebrew word for prophet, *nebi'im*, has no discernible linguistic connection with the Greek word *prophetes*. Yet hundreds of years after the Hebrew Bible was written, when the translators of the Septuagint were searching for a Greek word for the Hebrew *nebi'im*, they chose the word *prophetes*. Why? Evidently because the behavior and understanding of the Hebrew *nebi'im* (prophets) were similar to the behavior that Plato ascribed to the Greek *prophetes*.

It is significant that similar mannerisms and understandings of spirit possession were recorded in cultures that had little or no connection with each other. As we have shown in the last chapter, the phenomenon of spirit possession has been recorded in virtually every age, culture and religion. But when Plato recorded his observations of ecstatic prophecy in the ancient world, they were undoubtedly firsthand accounts, and thus they are very revealing. Plato calls the *prophetes* "madmen," but not in a pejorative sense. "Madness, when it comes from God, is superior to sanity, which is of human origin,"[12] he argued. He went on to describe inspired men, or ecstatics, as "men of God, men possessed by God, who without the aid of human reason utter important things. They are seized by the divinity and do not themselves know what they say, deprived as they are of ordinary understanding *being only mouthpieces of God*"[13] (emphasis mine).

"Madness" in the New Testament

Divinely inspired "madness" also exists in the New Testament. Almost four hundred years after Plato, we still find the concept of "spiritual madness," only now it is in the infant Corinthian church. First Corinthians 14:23 says that if "all speak in tongues, and ungifted men or unbelievers enter, will they not say '*mainesthe*'—you are mad?"

> The untranslated Greek verb in this location is commonly read as a pejorative statement and rendered "You are mad," thereby betraying modern estimates of ecstatic states. Aune points out that the verb most commonly used in Greek sources for the act of prophesying was *mainesthe*, which suggests that the Greek-speaking Corinthians would have understood this state **as an affirmation of divine inspiration**: "You are possessed"... prophecy effects the confession, "God is really among you."[14]

In context, Paul is correcting the Corinthian church for its excessive public use of tongues. In his correction Paul uses imagery that would have been common knowledge to the average Corinthian, namely that "madness" is associated with possession trance. Its use in this passage, however, is contrasted with prophecy. The point here is that the Corinthians did understand "madness" as spirit possession. "The response of the unbeliever to the community's collective speaking in tongues is to equate the Christian gathering with the mania that attended some of the mystery cults."[15] Tongues, therefore, used wrongly or in the wrong context, even though it is a gift from the Holy Spirit, could cause unbelievers to make untrue associations with the pagan possession trance experience. Paul's choice of the term *mainesthe* implies that his readers were aware of ecstasy in pagan cult worship. Add to this the fact that there was little *external* difference between the Corinthian believers and the pagan cult worshipers. Thus, all indications are that ecstatic experiences may look quite similar, regardless of whether they are divine or demonic in origin.

This was a pastoral concern to Paul. He wanted a clear, not a confused, signal in public meetings. He wanted understanding to be promoted in the Body, and so he noted that different functions should be performed at different times and places. Prophecy—which is intelligible—should be promoted in the corporate gatherings, and tongues in private.

The most significant point from this text for our purposes, however, is that Paul does not imply that this *mainesthe* is demonic. He says that it comes from the Holy Spirit. As a case in point, he acknowledges that he speaks in tongues more than any of them (see 1 Corinthians 14:18). He never comes close to suggesting that tongues, with its corresponding ecstasy, is "of the devil," as many modern Christians do. He does say that improper time and place can cause it to be misunderstood, but he never suggests that it is demonic. Ecstasy happens, and it comes from God. We need to make sure, therefore, that we pastor it wisely.

A Greater Power

This divinely inspired madness underscores that biblical prophets in both the Old and New Testaments were possessed by a power beyond themselves, and their behavior and corresponding ecstatic speech were evidently not of their own doing. The source of their inspiration was God Himself. God gave His prophets messages by overcoming them with His Spirit, and in ecstatic states they delivered what they received to the rest of His people.

The Israelites would have viewed their prophets, and the prophets would have viewed themselves, not as the source of the revelation, but rather as the mouthpieces through which the revelation flowed. They were messengers only, delivery boys—postmen, if you will (see Exodus 4:12, 13, 15; Numbers 23:5; Deuteronomy 18:18; Isaiah 59:21; Jeremiah 1:9). They had been undeniably overcome by One greater than themselves. They felt Him. They were shaken, trembled and had visions under His holy influence. They moved and had their being in Him, and then they obediently prophesied what they heard and saw, no matter what it cost them personally.

Indisputably, the personal lives of the prophets were adversely affected (they were stoned, put in prison, sawed in two, etc.) by the messages they delivered on behalf of Yahweh. This fact alone gives credence to the reality that the source of revelation came from outside of them. They had to have been possessed by a power beyond themselves. If they could have changed the content and/or the way in which they delivered the content in order to spare their lives, they undoubtedly would have. They knew the difference between their own thoughts and the messages they received while in ecstatic states. Something/Someone came upon them, and they were changed forever by the encounter.

The International Standard Bible Encyclopedia describes ecstasy this way:

> **Trance:** The condition expressed by this word is a mental state in which the person affected is *partially or wholly unconscious of objective sensations,* but intensely alive to subjective impressions which, however they may be originated, are felt

as if they were revelations from without. They may take the form of visual or auditory sensations or else of impressions of taste, smell, heat or cold, and *sometimes these conditions precede epileptic seizures constituting what is named the* aura epileptica.[16]

Let me repeat that wild statement! When the prophet goes into an ecstatic state to receive revelation from God, "sometimes these conditions precede epileptic seizures constituting what is named the *aura epileptica.*" It is clear that Holy Spirit possession, resulting in everything from mild trembling to wild shaking, is basic to a New Testament understanding of prophecy. Implicit in the rapturous descriptions of Acts 2, 2 Corinthians 12:1–3 and Revelation 4 is the understanding that spirit possession meant just that: The Holy Spirit came upon and possessed a human. This is how ecstasy would have been viewed in the cultural context of the early Church. I repeat: The issue of the day was not whether spirit possession occurred or not; rather, the issue was whether the spirit that possessed the person was divine or demonic.

I hope this study has not done to you what my New Testament exegesis class did to me—slightly bore you and make the dynamic truth somewhat dead. I want it to have the opposite effect: to make you desire the greater biblical experiences and to long for more of His presence in your life. Personally I love the fact that the works of God produce ecstasy. Everything He does produces awe, rapture and wonder. Ecstasy need not be feared, but it must be discerned. The closer we get to God, the more overpowered and overwhelmed we become by His presence. Every Christian should "eagerly desire . . . [above all other spiritual gifts] especially the gift of prophecy" (1 Corinthians 14:1, NIV), no matter in what form God chooses to release it.

5

Ecstasy—The Ways of God and the Mind of Man

God communicates throughout Scripture in a wide variety of ways. Sometimes when I read the Bible I smile or even laugh out loud at the bizarre ways God chooses to communicate. No wonder so many prophets were stoned to death! God commanded them to do the most peculiar things—things their contemporaries did not find to be holy or spiritual. In fact, the religious people of the day were infuriated by the prophets' simplicity, audacity and strangeness.

Often I hear people say, "God is a gentleman. He will not make you do anything you do not want to do." While this statement is true in some instances, such as salvation, it does not always reflect biblical reality. Both in the Bible and in times of revival, for example, God has overpowered men, and they did things they did not want to do. God has a history of confronting the traditions of men by ordering His prophets to act like fools. I now realize that often God has broken into human history in unusual and unfamiliar ways. From the stable (His birthplace of choice) to the cross (His chosen place of death),

God broke the expectations even of those with the greatest understanding of the Law and those closest to Him.

The foolishness of God is wiser than men. The ways of God are higher than ours.

The Birth of the Church

The most obvious example of the ways of God in regard to ecstasy is the birth of the Church. Can you imagine that God caused all of His apostles and leaders to look totally drunk in order to birth the Church? Yet the "drunkenness" and tongues that occurred with the birth of the Church were actually effects of ecstatic prophecy. (According to Peter's explanation in Acts 2:11, tongues was a form of prophecy whereby people prophesied, declaring the wonderful works of God in their own languages.)

> All of them were filled with the Holy Spirit and began to speak in other tongues as the Spirit enabled them. . . . "These men are not drunk, as you suppose. It's only nine in the morning! No, this is what was spoken by the prophet Joel: '"In the last days," God says, "I will pour out my Spirit on all people. Your sons and daughters will prophesy, your young men will see visions, your old men will dream dreams. Even on my servants, both men and women, I will pour out my Spirit in those days, and they will prophesy."'"
>
> Acts 2:4, 15–18, NIV

Ezekiel and Isaiah: Crazy Men?

The prophetic ways of God in the Old Testament were even more bizarre. I remember searching the Scriptures intently to find out what God viewed as "normal prophetic experience," and I could not believe what I read! Ezekiel, if he lived in our day, would be as ridiculed as he was in his own time, if not more so! One chapter alone, Ezekiel 4, describes how God asked Ezekiel to construct a miniature city, build ramparts around it, lay siege to it, lie on his side for 390 days next to it, then flip over for another forty days, all while eating nothing but grains cooked over human excrement! (Actually, after Ezekiel complained to God about the human excrement, God kindly allowed him to cook his food over cow dung [see Ezekiel 4:12–15].) If a prophet were to behave like this in a modern city or church, such a person would be admitted to a psychiatric hospital within a week—long before he fulfilled his prophetic assignment.

The great prophet Isaiah was instructed by God Himself to do something even crazier.

> At that time the LORD spoke through Isaiah the son of Amoz, saying, "Go and loosen the sackcloth from your hips and take your shoes off your feet." And he did so, *going naked and barefoot*. And the LORD said, "Even as My servant Isaiah has gone naked and barefoot three years as a sign and token against Egypt and Cush, so the king of Assyria will lead away the captives of Egypt and the exiles of Cush, young and old, naked and barefoot *with buttocks uncovered*, to the shame of Egypt."
>
> Isaiah 20:2–4, emphasis mine

Just imagine if today we saw a person walking around our city streets completely naked *for three and a half years!* Certainly none of us would go to the church he attended! Sometimes I like to quote this verse to critics and tell them that, even though I shake when I prophesy, at least I have always kept my clothes on! Pastors are always happy to hear that.

Mindsets Are Formed out of Personal Experience

The more I study God's Word and the more I observe my supernatural God moving in different nations and cultures, the more I am convinced that the worldviews or mindsets of most Christians are formed out of personal experience (or lack thereof!), rather than out of biblical understanding. And because we are finite and God is infinite, the expectations we form from personal experience actually limit our ability to know when God is speaking to us. In other words, because no prophet in my city has ever walked around naked for three and a half years and because my culture would label such behavior fringe and fanatical, my personal experience would condition me to say, "This cannot be God!" I would respond this way before talking to the prophet, testing what he has to say or praying to God myself, asking, "Is this You, God?"

Within Bible stories themselves, believers often react negatively, saying that what God is doing is not of God. Thomas, for example, responded, "Unless it happens to me, I will not believe that it could possibly be God!" (see John 20:25). How many of us have responded to the ways of God with similar attitudes?

Such attitudes place personal experience above biblical precedent. And the sad result is: We miss our day of visitation (see Luke 19:44).

In order to counteract man's tendency toward tradition formed from limited personal experiences, God often uses novel means to communicate eternal truth. He hates what the traditions of men can do to people (see Matthew 23:15). We must recognize, of course, that God did give certain traditions (such as wedding traditions, family traditions and special holy days) and without them we are very poor. And God did not change His mind in the New Testament regarding such traditions. But God's anger is against those who make void the Word of God by anti-Word traditions, through which people lose sight of the real intent of Scripture. He is also against those who develop traditions that prohibit the move of the Holy Spirit, and He despises it when people go through the motions but keep their hearts far from Him.

This truth was graphically illustrated to us in our Baptist church at one of our first prayer meetings after the Holy Spirit fell. God spoke to us strongly about how He feels about the traditions of men. He told us in no uncertain terms: *I spoke to you in My Word, and you did not listen. I brought prophetic people to you, and you did not listen. So now I am speaking to you like this* (i.e., strong manifestations and blowing) *so that you will do what I am asking you to do!* We have seen that God often uses ecstatic prophecy to get our attention and to help us become "doers of the word, and not hearers only, deceiving yourselves" (James 1:22, NKJV).

Possession Trance

Possessed by God. I like that phrase. This is how scholars describe the prophets.[1] They say that they were "possessed" by, or filled with, the Holy Spirit. Yet spirit possession in the Western world has largely been relegated to the "dark side." So in order to avoid confusion and add clarity when describing what happens to the biblical prophets, scholar David Aune replaces the words *spirit possession* or *ecstasy* with the more modern, descriptive phrase *revelatory trance.* He then divides the revelatory trance into two categories:

a. the vision trance (*seer* dimension), or

b. the possession trance (*nabi* dimension).[2]

These are significant descriptions of what happens to prophets when they are in states of ecstasy. Their experiences include both interior and exterior dimensions; in other words, when prophets begin to prophesy, stuff happens both inside and outside of them.

Several general distinctions should be made in the kinds of trance behavior characteristic of Israelite prophecy. First it is useful to distinguish between possession trance (which can be mediumistic) and vision trance. In possession trance it is believed that an external supernatural being or power has taken control of a person, while in the vision trance it is thought that the soul leaves the body or that it is subject to visions and hallucinations of various kinds. In the Old Testament, prophetic revelations are received by persons experiencing both types of trance. Second, *it is also useful to distinguish between controlled and uncontrolled possession.* Although initial experiences of a revelatory nature are often of an involuntary, uncontrolled and unpredictable nature (cf. 1 Samuel 10:6; 19:23–24), with practice religious specialists can learn to control subsequent experiences of trance (1 Samuel 10:5; 19:20).[3]

Dr. Aune raises an interesting point here. And I believe my personal experience sheds more light on the subject.

What Does It Feel Like to Be Possessed by God?

Many times I have been questioned about why I shake. I have been accused of everything from demon possession to immaturity ("When you are mature you will stop shaking") to attention-seeking ("Why do you have to do that? Are you just making it up?"). The implication is: "You should just prophesy without shaking." I have experienced a lot of internal struggle with the questions posed to me on whether "to shake or not to shake." And frankly, if ecstatic prophecy had not happened to me I would be asking the same questions. But since it has happened to me, let me tell you what ecstasy in prophesy feels like from an "insider's perspective."

When I begin to prophesy ecstatically I can actually feel the "spirit of prophecy" (Revelation 19:10) coming upon me. Often I feel a sensation from outside myself. I know it to be the presence of the Holy Spirit, but the Spirit of prophecy is quite distinct. I would compare it to what one sometimes feels in worship. While worshiping or praying some people can feel the manifest presence of God, and for no apparent reason they start weeping or become filled with joy. Of course they could stop the weeping by pulling themselves out of the presence that induces the weeping, but why would they want to? Similarly I can feel the presence of the "the Spirit of prophecy" coming upon me when I prophesy.

What happens on the outside and what happens on the inside of me during ecstatic prophecy are very different. Observers tell me they see a slight trembling on the outside of my body. My lips quiver, my eyelids flutter and for some reason unbeknownst to me a shaking begins in my feet and comes up my legs. It increases in intensity until I can no longer hold it back, and my head begins to shake violently from side to side, creating a wind sound that can be heard on the microphone if I am speaking into one. Depending upon intensity, I sometimes begin to twirl, jump and shout, all the while shaking violently, especially my head. For first time observers the external appearance of my ecstatic prophecy is quite shocking.

But inside I am intently focusing on God. Inside I feel completely calm, like the eye of a tornado. I go into a still, quiet place in the Holy Spirit, focusing on nothing but the presence of God. In this atmosphere Scripture verses and phrases begin to fill my mind. I am often overwhelmed in my soul with strong feelings. I can always tell if these feelings are from God (i.e., what God is feeling about a person or situation) or if they are from the atmosphere or the person for whom I am praying. I begin to feel God's heart. The Scriptures or words that come into my mind are accompanied by a "knowing" of how they apply to the person or situation. I often get other details as I start speaking. A flurry of information comes into my understanding, either through verses, phrases or pictures that I "see" in my mind's eye. I do not know how, but I almost always know what these pictures mean. As I speak these things, often certain words or phrases become accented by accompanying rushes of power. My voice gets louder, and the shaking intensifies. Although I am always aware of what I am saying, I have little or no control over these rushes of power, as they are completely uninitiated by me. I am generally so concentrating on what to say that I am oblivious to both my volume and the intensity of my shaking. Like I said, inside I feel calm and still and pure, like the eye of a storm. The whirlwind is outside of me.

People ask me if I ever hurt myself—my neck, my head, anything. The answer is no, not at any level. The shaking never hurts. I never get injured. The only thing that has been a problem is that my voice feels weak afterward. This is often the only indicator I have of how loud I have been speaking. But I am usually left with understandings of God and people that I did not have before the prophecy. It sometimes takes me days or weeks to give language to the deposit of understanding I have received about certain aspects of God's nature. This is why I spend a lot of time reading and praying the Bible. I want to find language for the revelation. And I always test my experience against Scripture.

What happens to me when I prophesy can be put into two categories: prophesying out of the gift and prophesying out of the presence of God. Sometimes I may begin by prophesying out of the spiritual gift of prophecy, which I can activate at will. When I, out of my own will,[4] activate the resident gift I experience no physical manifestations. Often, however, in the middle of prophesying out of the gift I can feel the Spirit of prophecy, or the presence of God, at a tangible level. Whenever this happens, even if I try to avoid it, I begin to shake.

The Psychology of Ecstasy

For the curious reader who wonders how all this works from a psychological point of view (I know there must be at least a few of you out there, since in my research for this book I came upon many writers who psychoanalyzed the physical manifestations of prophets and mystics), I thought I would add a psychological perspective to my study of ecstatic prophecy.

Frankly I also have been curious about the phenomenon, so I once asked a Christian leader who had a Ph.D. in psychology, "Why do I shake?" I told him about my internal struggle with the shaking aspect of prophecy and about the various critiques I had faced as a result. I asked him if there was a psychological reason for my shaking and whether or not he thought I could stop it.

The answer he gave me was similar to another point brought up by Dr. Aune, who said, "The revelatory trance exhibits a behavioral and experiential structure, which is socially communicated and 'learned' by those who have had such apparently 'spontaneous' experiences."[5] The point is that the initial, "spontaneous" experience can be repeated and exhibits patterns of learned behavior. The psychologist expounded upon this. He told me that the brain patterns itself around powerful experiences, and the synapses in the brain connect according to the stimuli to which the body is exposed. This is a well-known psychological fact and has been recorded in experiments, such as the world-renowned experiment with "Pavlov's dog."[6]

The psychologist explained to me that the manifest presence of God is an exterior stimulus. Spiritually sensitive persons can feel God's presence in a tangible way. When a prophet, therefore, has a powerful encounter with the Spirit of God in which he/she has been bodily overcome by His presence, the initial experience leaves imprints on the patterns of the brain. The synapses connect, setting off corresponding physical responses to the presence of God. He explained to me that this is commonly understood by psychiatrists. If a girl, for example, has been abused and her abuser always wore the same cologne, then forever after—even into adulthood—when the woman smells that certain cologne her body will unconsciously freeze and go into a set pattern of behavior. The association between the cologne and the abuse creates patterns in the brain, automatically setting off corresponding physical reactions. This phenomenon works with both positive and negative experiences. Positive experiences (i.e., association between food and drooling in the case of Pavlov's dogs) also create patterns in the brain that set off bodily responses. Biblically, it is evident that Holy Spirit possession causes the human body to have physiological responses. I find it highly interesting that in the Bible similar exterior behavior is recorded in prophetic encounters that took place centuries apart from one another. Evidently there are physical reactions to the manifest presence of God.

Lessons from the Life of Ezekiel

One of my more famous prophecies, "Eyes & Wings," was birthed out of a long season of seeking the Lord after being confronted by people I highly respected about the issue of shaking. The confrontation left me troubled and confused. I am fully aware of how weird it looks to outsiders. At that time I had no answers as to why I shook when I prophesied. I felt embarrassed, and worse, I felt that perhaps I was bringing disrepute or dishonor to the name of the Lord. I am acutely cognizant of the fact that, in the Western world at least, what happens to me is fringe behavior. This awareness has caused me to try to control and/or stop the shaking at numerous times in my life. I often wished I could be like Daniel, a prophet with some dignity, instead of like Ezekiel—a prophet who was so weird. But God gives gifts as He chooses (see 1 Corinthians 12:11) and that serve His purposes, and sometimes the choice is not ours to make.

Since I desire only to please God always, I went to the Lord and asked Him, "Please talk to me about why I do this. I need to know who I am in You, and who You are in me. I want to understand why I do this." In answer to my questions, God led me to spend several months in the first few chapters of the book of Ezekiel. I prayed through Ezekiel's calling, studied how God came upon him, looked at what God asked him to do and meditated on how Ezekiel must have looked from the outside. I sought to learn why God made His prophets act bizarrely and offensively in front of the rest of His people. I must admit that I found a lot of solace in this study. And I learned a great deal about the ways of God.

The image of an Old Testament priest—a consecrated man—in his thirtieth year sitting by the river Chebar having visions of God stuck in my mind. Ezekiel's life was altered dramatically by his visionary experiences. Something happened to Ezekiel when he saw God—something that caused him to obey every command, even to the point of going to the center of his city, building a miniature city out of wood blocks, then lying down next to it in the same spot for well over a year, eating grains cooked over cow dung. Why would God ask His servant to do such repugnant acts? What does this tell us about the ways of God? It tells us a lot.

We are following a God who is in love with us. He is far more passionate about us than we are about Him. He loves. Consequently, He also hates:

> I *hate* your new moon festivals and your appointed feasts, they have become a burden to Me; I am weary of bearing them.
>
> Isaiah 1:14–15, emphasis mine

> I *hate*, I *reject* your festivals, nor do I delight in your solemn assemblies.
>
> Amos 5:21–22, emphasis mine

It pains God to give so freely and fully to His people (even giving His beloved Son) and yet to be spurned repeatedly in return. He laments in the book of Ezekiel, "How I have been hurt by their adulterous hearts which turned away from Me, and by their eyes, which played the harlot after their idols" (Ezekiel 6:9). How empty it is for God when people say the right words but their hearts are far from Him! The heart behind our words—this is what the Spirit is searching to know. Although God knows our hearts, it is we who often are blinded to what is in them. So God sends His prophets to shake things up. He offends our minds to reveal our hearts. It is through the base things, the foolish things, that God makes Himself known. The cradles, the crosses and the prophets have a lot in common. Their deep message is hidden in simple, obscure and even irrational things. Only those who search will find Him in them.

Touching the Heart of God

When prophets are possessed by God, they have a whole new level of empathetic understanding of God's emotions. They carry His feelings within them and often speak of them in first person. The spiritual experiences of the prophets cause them actually to touch the heart of God. From then on they are marked by the feelings of God and carry them deeply in their spirits wherever they go. They cannot look at life and society the same after God possesses them. Their vantage point shifts from how *society* feels to how *God* feels. Because of His jealous love for mankind, God's emotions are deeply affected by the lives of His children on earth.

An analysis of prophetic utterances shows that the fundamental experience of the prophet is a *fellowship with the feelings of God*, a *sympathy with the divine pathos*, a communion with the divine consciousness which comes about through the prophet's reflection of, or participation in, the divine pathos. The typical prophetic state of mind is one of being taken up into the heart of the divine pathos. Sympathy is the prophet's answer to inspiration, the correlative to revelation.

The emotional experience of the prophet becomes the focal point for the prophet's understanding of God. He lives not only in his personal life, but also in the life of God. The prophet hears God's voice and feels His heart. He tries to impart the pathos of the message together with the logos.[7]

By divine command prophets live in circumstances that cause them to feel the feelings of God firsthand. Either from a possession trance experience or from living a parallel vicarious lifestyle (see Ezekiel 24:15–19; and the Book of Hosea), prophets connect with the feelings of God very deeply. Their obedience to His commands, with the subsequent rejection by the masses, bonds them to God. The prophets are His bondservants (see Revelation 11:18; 22:6). They feel how He feels when He is rejected. They fellowship with His sufferings (see Philippians 3:10). They are His friends. From the outside they are ridiculed. But inside they know Him, because through revelation, ecstasy and lifestyle He has made His heart known to them.

Carrying God's Word in Different Ways

A cursory reading of Scripture shows that different prophets "carried" the word of the Lord in different ways. Jeremiah was emotionally affected, the prophets in Samuel's school were physically affected and the lifestyles of Hosea and Ezekiel were affected. Each prophet carried God's words in different ways, but God spoke through them all. And those who listened to the prophets heard God's heart behind the emotions, the manifestations and the lifestyles.

As I studied Ezekiel and prayed through it, I grew stronger inside. I became more confident with the person God made me to be and with how He asked me to carry His words. I love that He shares His heart with me, and I feel privileged to see the world more as He sees it. If I had not felt God as tangibly as I have, I know I would lack much of the spiritual knowledge I have now. I have learned things from the Spirit—even from the way the Spirit moves on me—that have enriched my understanding of the Word and caused me to know God better.

6

CAN ECSTASY BE CONTROLLED OR INDUCED?

Mostly I have given up judging by appearance. Only God knows the heart. So when I am tempted to reject something with which I am unfamiliar—or someone with whom I am unfamiliar—I force myself to take a deep breath and ask a few more questions. I now ask, "What is in the heart? What is the reason these methods were employed?" Taking time to look beyond the surface has served me well.

At one youth conference I attended, the person taking tickets at the entrance had piercings all over his body. At my age I have a hard time understanding why people do that to themselves. Those from my era and culture tend to think that people with multiple body piercings are strange. But here I was at a Christian youth conference, and this pierced young man was taking tickets, which meant he was on our side!

In addition to the piercing on his ears, eyes and upper lip, the young man had a tongue ring. I thought I would just "go there" with him, so I asked, "Hey, did it hurt to put that piercing in your tongue?"

"Yeah, but not as much as it hurt to pierce my nipple," he responded, lifting his shirt to show me the evidence.

Inside I was thinking, *That is more information than I asked for*, but I decided that since he was direct with me I would be direct with him. "So why did you get all that piercing anyway? What made you want to do that to yourself?"

The young man gave me a surprising answer. "You know in the Bible where it says that if you want to be a bond-slave of God you need to get your ear pierced? Well, I just wanted God to have all of me: my speech, my vision, my heart. So I pierced everything." Although this is not an endorsement for body piercing, I was impressed with the amount of desire the young man's answer demonstrated. It showed me yet once more that motivation—what is in the heart—is the most important thing.

The Prophet Is Not His Own

This illustration and principle have some bearing on ecstatic prophecy. One cannot always tell from the outside what is happening inside a person. Shaking can have a demonic source, a fleshly source or a divine source. Outsiders may have numerous opinions about what is going on and why such behavior is occurring. In fact, dozens and dozens of books analyze the prophets and mystics of the Church from a psychological point of view. Everyone wants an explanation for the exterior behavior.

Many times outsiders have challenged me with Scripture, such as, "The spirits of prophets are subject to prophets" (1 Corinthians 14:32). The assumption from this text is that the prophet can control the behavior. But this is not always the case. The Bible repeatedly speaks of prophetic experiences where the prophets were overcome, could not stand, became like dead men, had no strength, etc. They could not control what happened to them physically in possession trance experiences. Nor did they have any choice about the means of communicating the revelation God gave them: "Ezekiel, your wife, whom you love, is going to die tonight as a sign to Israel, and you cannot mourn about it" (Ezekiel 24:16, paraphrased). "Jeremiah, you think you can control this, but I will burn this word in you from the inside out until you have to say it" (Jeremiah 20:9, paraphrased).

I testify as well that the prophet cannot always control the behavior, especially when ecstasy intensifies. Sometimes I cannot control the shaking.

> For each time I speak, I cry aloud; I proclaim violence and destruction, because for me the word of the LORD has resulted in reproach and derision all day long. But if I say, "I will not remember Him or speak anymore in His name," *then in my heart it becomes like a burning fire shut up in my bones; and I am weary of holding it in, and I cannot endure it.*
>
> Jeremiah 20:8–9, emphasis mine

Because of the "reproach and derision" of carrying the word of the Lord ecstatically, in some seasons of my life I have determined, "I will not shake." During these seasons I have concentrated fully on prophesying without manifestations. Once I actually did succeed in not shaking for about eight months. The problem, however, was that I stopped prophesying, too. I was concentrating so hard on not shaking that all my energy was focused there, and the prophetic gift completely shut down in my life. Why? I think it is because I actually stopped the flow or "the carrying of" the Spirit. Like the illustration of weeping, I was pulling myself out of the presence before weeping would come. I tried to control God's "taking me." And prophecy reignited in me only when I went back to the Lord and said, "Whatever You want, however You want to use me, I surrender." I am not my own; I am bought with a price.

"Subject to the Prophets"

This interior dimension of the prophet must be explored not by theorists but by the practitioners themselves. Yes, the Bible says, "The spirit of the prophets is subject to the prophets." But what does that mean? First of all, let's look at that verse in its context.

> What is the outcome then, brethren? When you assemble, each one has a psalm, has a teaching, has a revelation, has a tongue, has an interpretation. Let all things be done for edification. If anyone speaks in a tongue, it should be by two or at the most three, and each in turn, and one must interpret; but if there is no interpreter, he must keep silent in the church; and let him speak to himself and to God. Let two or three prophets speak, and let the others pass judgment. But if a revelation is made to another who is seated, the first one must keep silent. For you can all prophesy one by one, so that all may learn and all may be exhorted; and the spirits of prophets are subject to prophets; for God is not a God of confusion but of peace.
>
> 1 Corinthians 14:26–33

The entire context of this Scripture is the regulation of the gifts in the Church. In the Corinthian church the Holy Spirit flowed so strongly that when they assembled together everyone had a psalm, a teaching, a revelation, a tongue, an interpretation (verse 26). Paul was attempting to bring some order to services where everyone was talking over one another.

Having been in hundreds of meetings where the Spirit is flowing, I understand completely what Paul is addressing here. When the "Spirit of prophecy" enters a room everyone receives revelation. And if a church lets it, the prophecy will flow for hours at a time. Much of the prophetic revelation is confirming; it is God saying the same thing in a hundred different ways—through pictures, tongues, prophecy, songs and trances. Just as in Samuel's school of the prophets, most people in the room or region start prophesying, whether they have ever done so before or not.

The Corinthians were letting prophecy rule their meetings. Paul corrected this by saying that prophecy has its place, but the corporate services must make room for all components: worship (our talking to God), prophecy (God responding), teaching, fellowship, breaking of bread and prayer. Paul said prophets should function in the service—but only two or three of them. It is clear from the context that not every revelation needs to be delivered in one meeting. Once two or three prophets have spoken, the church is directed to continue with the rest of the service, making room for the other elements.

So, yes, the spirit of the prophet is subject to the prophet in this way: The prophet does not have to give every revelation he/she has. In a corporate meeting, let a couple of prophets speak, and then go on with the service. But *do* let two or three prophets speak in church.

Paul is not necessarily limiting prophecy to two or three in the whole meeting. Neither is Paul saying we should have no prophecy. On the contrary (and he gives these instructions after 1 Corinthians 13:8–12), we should make way for prophecy when we assemble together. Prophecy is the testimony of Jesus Himself (see Revelation 19:10) and therefore is an essential ingredient of New Testament church services. But do not let one gift take over a corporate meeting. Paul makes it clear that "you all can prophesy in turn." People should prophesy each revelation one at a time, and then make room for other manifestations of the Spirit to flow.

The prophet, then, has a choice. He does have a will and a say in *when* and *where* he prophesies. I know that I have a choice in *when* and *where* I prophesy. Jonah had a choice (well, sort of). Jeremiah had a choice. Every prophet has a choice as to whether he will let God use him to prophesy or not. He can choose to surrender to the Spirit of prophecy and therefore when and where he will deliver that prophecy. In other words, the prophet can either permit or oppose surrender to the Spirit of prophecy. When the ecstatic prophet chooses to surrender to the Spirit, God then takes over and the prophet is subject to *how* God wishes to communicate. But not to prophesy ever is disobedience (see Ezekiel 33:1–20).

Fleshly Manifestations

Not every manifestation is either divine or demonic. There is a third possibility. Some manifestations are fleshly.

Generally, fleshly manifestations are the most difficult to deal with. They distract people from what God is doing and attract attention to themselves. I have led hundreds of prophetic meetings, led the prophetic department of a church and built national prophetic roundtables. In the course of all this prophecy I have seen more than my fair share of fleshly manifestations. To use a metaphor from the book of Jude, I have seen a lot of "clouds without water" (verse 12). In other words, the manifestation appears real, but it has no substance.

When I lead prophetic meetings and people begin to manifest but give no evident reason for the manifestations to the rest of the group, I usually ask such people to leave the room. Paul's correction to the Corinthians indicates that some clear "sound" or intelligible reason for such behavior must be given to the whole group, or else the prophet should not speak: "If there is no interpretor, the speaker should keep quiet" (1 Corinthians 14:28, NIV). This principle means that if manifestations occur for no apparent reason, then the person should "keep quiet" or in this case stop the manifestation. I discuss this in greater detail in chapter 10 when I address "Ecstasy in the Assembly." But suffice it to say here that the goal is to have a clear sound (see 1 Corinthians 14:7–8), and manifestations that do not produce a clear sound in a public context should not be allowed or, at best, should be monitored closely.

Yet I know that some things do happen from the Holy Spirit. In other words, we may not yet understand what is happening, but the Spirit is still moving. I regularly pray, as Moses did, "Teach me your ways" (Exodus 33:13), and I have found God to be faithful to answer that prayer. The Holy Spirit "guides us into all truth" (see John 16:13), so we do not need to react or be afraid of new things or unfamiliar ways. If I am leading a meeting and am uncertain of a manifestation, I generally operate on the principle of letting the wheat and the tares grow together. It will eventually become known whether what is operating is the Spirit, the flesh or the devil, and my feeling is that the wheat is too precious to lose on account of a few tares. True Holy Spirit ecstasy will always be a catalyst to cause people to return to God's intent for them.

Can Ecstasy Be Induced?

In the Bible, external stimuli aid and abet the inducement of revelatory states.

> Scholars have often emphasized the artificial nature of the "ecstasy" induced by prophets in the Old Testament. "Ecstasy," or the revelatory trance as we prefer to call it, is said to have been induced through the rhythmical beat of music (see 1 Samuel 10:5; 2 Kings 3:15), dancing (see 1 Kings 18:21), group excitement (see Numbers 11:24–30; 1 Samuel 10:5–13; 19:20–24) and self-flagellation (see 1 Kings 18:28–29; Zechariah 13:6). It is certainly true that the revelatory trance can be induced by these and other methods.[1]

> It must be recognized that what many modern scholars have pejoratively designated as "artificially induced ecstasy" was never criticized or regarded as illegitimate by the ancient Israelites. Further, the few references which have been interpreted as trance induction do not bear the weight assigned to them. . . . Further, the verbs *hitnabbe'* and *nibba'* in 1 Samuel 10:5, 6, 10; 19:20, 21, 23, usually translated "prophesy," should

probably be rendered "rave." The behavior of prophets was sometimes labeled as drunkenness (Isaiah 28:7) or madness (Hosea 9:7; 2 Kings 9:11; Jeremiah 29:26; 1 Samuel 16:14–16, 23; 18:10–11).[2]

The Bible does seem to legitimize what Dr. Aune says above. Dancing, although not directly mentioned in conjunction with the Israelite prophets, was an important part of the worship experience in both Israelite and Baal worship, and because of this "we are entitled to assume that the primitive prophets also used dancing to evoke ecstasy."[3] The harpist aided Elisha in hitting a revelatory state (see 2 Kings 3:15). The disciples waited in prayer for many days in a row in the Upper Room until the Holy Spirit fell and they prophesied ecstatically.

As we discussed in the previous chapter, false prophets also used similar means to hit ecstatic states. Does this mean that dancing, music and waiting on God are "artificial" means of producing ecstasy and/or revelation? I think not!

I believe that revelation is the fruit of relationship. As we talk to God through prayer, worship and praise such as that expressed in passionate dance, He talks back. Pursuit begets response. I do not believe that the issue is whether or not the prophetic ecstasy was artificially induced, unless of course the "prophets" have used artificial intoxicants, such as drugs or alcohol. No, I believe that the real issue is which deity is being invoked and which deity is talking back.

Ecstatic Prophecy Draws Us Closer to God

Everything that comes out of a Holy Spirit-initiated ecstatic encounter involves a heightened awareness of God—the God of the Bible. It has been my personal experience that ecstasy, when it comes from God, serves only to bring us to a greater understanding of who He is and how He thinks. Many times when I feel ecstasy come upon me, not only do I receive revelation about others whom I do not know, but I also receive revelation about Jesus that I did not previously know. I have learned so much about God from the times He has come upon me. As a result, I understand why prophecy is a "greater gift" and why we should eagerly desire it, especially in its highest forms.

7

ECSTATIC PROPHECY
IN CHURCH HISTORY

The heroes of the hall of faith recorded in Hebrews 11 all were commended for the way their faith moved them to action. Their actions produced a testimony. The first hero mentioned in this hall of faith was Abel, the second child of Adam:

> By faith Abel offered God a better sacrifice than Cain did. By faith he was commended as a righteous man, when God spoke well of his offerings. And by faith he still speaks, even though he is dead.
>
> Hebrews 11:4, NIV

Though Abel had been dead and gone for thousands of years, the author of Hebrews credits him with "still" speaking. The same is true of all those who have died in Christ. In a real way their testimonies still speak today, and they form an ongoing salvation history of the work of God upon the earth.

The speech of the Christian dead is a major test and affirmation of whether or not ecstatic prophecy is from God. The reasoning is simple. Scripture does not describe everything God can or does do in His people (see John 20:30). In order to verify the spiritual source of prophetic ecstasy, it must therefore be tested by doctrine (what is confessed about Christ) and fruit (what is produced for Christ). It also can be tested by comparing it with what God has done previously in Church history. If the same types of experiences have happened in the lives of godly people in other ages and other places and the corporate testimony of Church history is congruent with the present testimonies, then it is safe to affirm that "the Lord has done this, and it is marvelous in our eyes" (Matthew 21:42, NIV).

We should not expect, however, the same manifestations to occur at every place in every time. The fact that they occur at all is testimony enough. Israel, for instance, was in bondage under Egypt for four hundred years, and during that time they waited for a visitation from God. Maybe whole generations came and went with no word from heaven. On the other hand, prophetic activity and the phenomena of God evidently took place from the time of Samuel to the time of Elisha. These appear to have happened on a regular basis within a prophetic community. It is not the regularity that authenticates an issue, then, but the fact that it happens at all. A thousand testimonies from people who doubt that God heals are silenced with just a couple of authentic, documented healings. Two or three exceptions to the rule prove that it is not a rule. Smatterings of accounts are accounts enough. And with respect to phenomena associated with prophetic activity, the research of Church archives and historical data is illuminating such an abundance of accounts that one hardly knows where to begin.

Evidence of a Mighty Move of God

Historical accounts of manifestations are evidenced during what we now know were heightened times of God's salvation work. Testimonies abound to confirm that ecstasy occurred during the first and second Great Awakenings, during the Welsh and Azusa Street revivals and during many other recognized moves of the Holy Spirit. In his timely book *When the Spirit Comes with Power*, Dr. John White concluded that the regularity of phenomena linked to revivals proved that manifestations of the Spirit are an evidence of a heightened move of God.[1]

The Roman Catholic Church (the dominant church up until the 1500s) records ecstasy as occurring for hundreds of years and provides a clear historical definition of it in the Church's encyclopedia. Strikingly, the definition is similar to the theological assessments of biblical ecstasy that we have already addressed.

> Supernatural ecstasy may be defined as a state, which, while it lasts, includes two elements:
>
> - the one, interior and invisible, when the mind rivets its attention on a religious subject [i.e., what David Aune calls "the revelatory trance"].
> - the other, corporeal and visible, when the activity of the senses is suspended, so that not only are external sensations incapable of influencing the soul, but considerable difficulty is experienced in awakening such sensation, and this whether the ecstatic himself desires to do so, or others attempt to quicken the organs into action [i.e., what David Aune calls "the possession trance"].
>
> That quite a large number of the saints have been granted ecstasies is attested by hagiology; and nowadays even freethinkers *are slow to deny historical facts that rest on so solid a basis.*[2]

The Corporate Witness of Church History

No matter where and when one looks into Church history, accounts of ecstatic prophecy are evident and accompany mighty moves of God. In the Bible, almost every occurrence of ecstatic prophecy takes place with groups of people, and this is also true within Church history. Also in the Bible the Spirit of prophecy is transferable (i.e., Moses to the seventy elders in Numbers 11:25–27; Elijah to his servant Gehazai and to Elisha in 1 Kings 19; Acts 2; and through the laying on of hands). This is commonly observed in almost every prophetic movement throughout Church history as well. Let's start near the beginning.

1. Montanists

Montanism was a prophetic movement within Christianity that began during the third quarter of the second century and subsequently spread to all corners of the Greco-Roman world. Montanism is classic ecstatic prophecy. It spread like wildfire after its founder, Montanus, had a powerful revelatory experience. It is an observable pattern that whenever ecstasy occurs throughout the centuries, the Church debates its legitimacy. Montanism is no exception. Eusebius, one of the early Church fathers, quotes an unknown opponent of Montanism, who provides an account of the origins of this movement. The account is filled with biased and derogatory statements, casting an opinionated shadow on its validity.

In Phrygian Mysia there is said to be a village called Ardabau. There they say that a recent convert called Montanus . . . *became obsessed and suddenly fell into frenzy and convulsions.* He began to be ecstatic and to speak and to talk strangely, prophesying *contrary to the custom which belongs to the tradition and succession of the Church* from the beginning. . . . But by some art, or rather by such an evil scheme of artifice, the devil wrought destruction for the disobedient, and receiving unworthy honours from them stimulated and inflamed their understanding which was already dead to the true faith; so that he raised up two more women and filled them with the bastard spirit so that they spoke madly and improperly and strangely like Montanus. The spirit gave blessings to those who rejoiced and were proud in him and puffed them up by the greatness of its promises.[3]

But is this an accurate assessment of what really took place? Obviously two people can observe the same event and give completely different explanations, depending upon their worldview or theological vantage point. Aune, commenting on Eusebius' negative reaction to Montanist prophecy, says:

> Eusebius and his sources are obviously very critical of Montanus and the movement which he began. They impugn his motives and describe his and his followers' possession trance experiences with terminology drawn from pagan divination. This deliberate attempt by Christian heresiologists to paganize Montanus has led many modern scholars to agree that Montanist prophecy was an intrusion of pagan revelatory ecstasy into Christianity. *This view is completely false.* All of the major features of early Montanism, including the behaviour associated with possession trance, are derived from early Christianity. Montanism is particularly associated with the Gospel of John and the Apocalypse of John . . . In general, *Montanism should be viewed as a renewal movement* within the second-century Church.[4]

In sharp contrast to Eusebius, Tertullian (another early Church father) strongly endorsed Montanist prophecy, referring to its oracles as "oracles of the Spirit." Tertullian writes about the accounts of *The Visions of Perpetua*, an early Christian martyr, enthusiastically approving them. He was convinced they came from God, and the prophecies did bear out to be true in real life. In the visions, Perpetua, a godly young Christian woman, foresaw her martyrdom, described it in detail and subsequently lived it.

The traditional Church had problems with Montanism, at least in part, because of the Montanist position on an ethical lifestyle. To acknowledge the Montanist prophets' veracity would have put a demand on the greater Church to live a more holy life. But this is precisely why Tertullian endorsed the Montanists. He saw the compromise creeping into the Church of his day and recognized the need for change.

He had grown angry at what looked like compromise creeping into the Church—unwillingness to be martyred, willingness to forgive more serious public sins—and aligned himself with the Montanists. It is unclear whether this involved actually leaving the Church, but his later works are avowedly Montanist, and one or two explicitly attack the mainstream Church on these points. As such he was not recognized as a Saint, despite his orthodoxy, and his works were all marked as condemned in the sixth century *Decretum Gelasianum*.[5]

Tertullian was a brilliant apologist and was unabashed in his endorsement of prophecy. Though the traditions of men had already taken root in the churches of his day, Tertullian always acknowledged the need for the dynamic work of the Holy Spirit, some of which came through prophecies and dreams.

And thus we—who *both acknowledge and reverence, even as we do the prophecies, modern visions as equally promised to us and consider the other powers of the Holy Spirit as an agency of the Church* for which also He was sent, administering all gifts in all, even as the Lord distributed to every one as well—needfully collect them in writing, as we commemorate them in reading to God's glory.[6]

2. Quakers

If we fast-forward many hundred years and cross a few nations, then we discover another ecstatic prophetic movement: the Quakers. Why do you think they were called "Quakers"? This is not a trick question. The answer is obvious: because they quaked! Whenever the Holy Spirit came upon them, they shook and trembled so visibly that their critics could see it. Thus, they were named, and they never got rid of the label. It was their trademark.

The Quaker movement was an orthodox movement that began in the 1600s in England while the nation was suffering tremendous religious and political upheaval. Many people during that season of suffering, particularly the poor, began proclaiming that they received miracles, prophecies and shaking ecstasy. George Fox is credited as the founder of this movement, which grew to sixty thousand adherents in the first decade. Fox's followers were called Quakers because of the violent trembling that came upon them when they worshiped. One of their own elders wrote about their reasons for quaking.

> Quaker missionaries risked death and imprisonment to persuade others to become Friends of the Truth. . . . Our Quaker forebears quaked because the light shone on their sins and shortcomings, and they took seriously Jesus' command that we be "perfect as our heavenly Father is perfect." They called themselves Friends because Jesus told his followers, "You are my friends if you do whatsoever I command you" (John 15:15).
>
> It was not at all the early Quakers' purpose to establish an alternative to the Church, but rather to purify the practice of religion. As Fox wrote, "None can make better than the pure undefiled religion, which was set up in the Church in the apostles' days."[7]

When the phenomena of quaking engulfed them, the Quakers would prophesy and preach from the Bible, because they believed that the "inner light" of the indwelling Holy Spirit would reveal the truth of the Scriptures. The prophecies delivered through the Quakers were often aimed at societal change. Quaker women would preach in public places, denouncing corruption and complacency. Their emphasis on purity and righteousness caused them to be ridiculed as fanatics and increased their persecution.

Here is an excerpt from George Fox's journal, describing the type of manifestations happening at that time:

> Being set at liberty, I went to the inn where Captain Drury, . . . [who] was an enemy to me and to the Truth, and opposed

it . . . While I was under his custody, and he was by, he would
scoff at trembling, and call us Quakers, as the Independents
and Presbyterians had nicknamed us before. But afterward
he came and told me that, as he was lying on his bed to rest
himself in the daytime, a sudden trembling seized on him;
that his joints knocked together, and his body shook so that
he could not rise from his bed. He was so shaken that he had
not strength enough left to rise. But he felt the power of the
Lord was upon him; and he tumbled off his bed, and cried
to the Lord, and said he would never speak more against the
Quakers, such as trembled at the word of God.[8]

Without a doubt "George Fox and the Quakers believed
themselves to be prophets . . . [and] made prophesying the
very center of their worship."[9] They equated their inspiration with that of Isaiah, Amos, Jeremiah and Ezekiel. They
quaked, walked naked and barefoot and used a variety of signs
and symbols to denounce the corruption that existed in both
Church and state. Their enthusiasm infuriated those in power,
and they were cruelly persecuted as a result.

It did not take long for the ecstatic Quakers, or Friends, as
they called themselves, to be called witches and heretics.
It did not matter that the Quakers quoted the Bible to de-
fend their quaking, pointing out that Moses "quaked," David
"roared," and Jeremiah "trembled." They were still found guilty
of harboring evil ways. Some were dunked, bridled, whipped,
bored through the tongue with a hot iron, branded on the
forehead with the letter B (for blasphemer) and sent to jail.
As persecution continued over the years, the Quakers gave
up their ecstatic and prophetic role in society and changed to
being calm advocates of education and organized meetings.
The quaking stopped, along with their persecution. . . . And
all Quakers throughout the world have essentially stopped
quaking.

I believe that the Quakers stopped quaking because they
were persecuted, even imprisoned, for their wild ecstatic experiences. When they were obedient to the truth of ecstatic

expression, they were unable to stop quaking. Quaker and syndicated columnist David Yount wrote an essay in 2002 asking the question, "Why Did Quakers Stop Quaking?" Yount ended his essay by quoting an elder Quaker in his eighties who gave this response: "I know why I don't quake. I don't ask God the hard questions about what He requires me to do with my life. I'm afraid that if I ask Him, God will tell me something difficult that I'm unwilling to do. But if I was willing to listen to Him and do what He demands, then I'd start quaking."[10]

I can relate to this gentleman's testimony. The stigma associated with quaking caused persecution, which caused Quakers to shut down the gift from the inside. Unfortunately, as the testimony of the eighty-year-old elder points out, obedience to the will of God stopped when he stopped asking God "the hard questions." I know many people who were birthed in ecstatic prophecy during heightened moves of the Spirit who purposefully shut down the gift. The stigma associated with shaking was too much, and it was easier to give up prophesying than it was to carry the gift with this manifestation.

There are other possible reasons, however, that the Quakers stopped quaking. As I mentioned, doctrine is often formed out of experience. The Quaker doctrine of moving according to the "inner light" restricted them *not* to move when there was no "stirring of the waters" (a Quaker term for the manifestation of the presence of God). Thus, they still wait for this stirring—and the manifestation of quaking that accompanies it—before they speak in a meeting. This means that they wait in quietude until someone quakes or "is stirred." Unless this happens, they will not even preach the Bible. Their reasoning is: "If the Spirit does not move, then we will not move." This could be another reason for their steep decline in influence. People should not take such extreme positions. Quaking or no quaking, the Bible always speaks, and we can always hear God speaking to us when we read it. Doctrines should not be made about manifestations, for even when manifestations do occur they are merely signs pointing to a greater reality.

3. The French Calvinist Huguenots

Almost simultaneous with the Quaker revival in England was the ecstatic prophetic Huguenot movement in France. Formally organized in 1559, it was a genuine evangelical move. The group was exceedingly persecuted from the beginning, and when King Louis XIV issued an edict in 1685 banning Protestantism, the Huguenots were virtually annihilated. They suffered force, violence, and moral and physical torture, and they were forced to renounce their faith or die.

What is interesting to us about this movement is that it was almost entirely ecstatic in nature. This is an undisputed fact. Below is a critic's assessment of what happened in Huguenot meetings:

> Respecting the physical manifestations, there is little discrepancy between the accounts of friend and foe. The persons affected were men and women, the old and the young. Very many were children, boys and girls of nine or ten years of age. They were sprung from the people—their enemies said, from the dregs of the people—ignorant and uncultured; for the most part unable to read or write. . . .
>
> Such persons would suddenly fall backward and, while extended at full length on the ground, undergo strange and apparently involuntary contortions; their chests would seem to heave, their stomachs to inflate. On coming gradually out of this condition, they appeared instantly to regain the power of speech. Beginning often in a voice interrupted by sobs, they soon poured forth a torrent of words—cries for mercy, calls to repentance, exhortations to the bystanders to cease frequenting the mass, denunciations of the church of Rome, prophecies of coming judgment.[11]

Any student of revival will recognize that transferable ecstasy is almost always a major component of revival. The Huguenot movement is no exception. The Spirit of prophecy seemed to hit anyone who came into the Huguenots' geographical area.

The Huguenot movement actually began as a school of the prophets. A man by the name of Duserre began a prophetic school, where many of the students were as young as ten to twelve years old. Training included intensive ministry time, prayer, fasting and teaching of the Word. The students became filled with the Spirit, prophesied, had ecstatic experiences, fell to the ground, worshiped and trembled under the power of God. After this they were sent out, and wherever they went prophecy burst into flame. They were said to have left "traces" because people received the "graces"; in other words, people received the prophetic gift, and it seemed that almost everyone began to prophesy. It was said that the valleys were swarming with prophets and the mountains were filled with *les inspirés*, or "the inspired ones."

One of the Huguenots' most inveterate opponents, a man named Brueys, had a theory about their manifestations:

Abbot Brueys (a former Protestant converted by Bossuet) has a medical theory: "It is an illness of the spirit, a kind of melancholy. Their minds are deranged by fasts, prayer watches and fatigue." But he also suspects that the pastors in exile are behind things, singling out weak minds to make Protestants rise up against the authorities. He speaks of DuSerre and his "prophet factory," accusing him of teaching the children "posturing, foolish antics, hand clapping, throwing themselves backward on the ground, closing their eyes, swelling their stomachs and throats, remaining dormant in that state and then, on waking up with a start, uttering out loud everything which came into their mouths."[12]

The interesting thing is that up until that time, the Church of the day was traditional and regimented, the women and children were silent, and the lay people had no Bibles. But now the Holy Spirit was being poured out on everyone—the old and the young, the men and the women (kind of like Acts 2). Initially this was good, and much good fruit came from it. Revival broke out, and thousands of conversions occurred as a result.

Over time, however, things began to go awry. As with the Quakers, the anointing led the service, not the Word. Prophets took the place of teachers. Leadership was replaced by manifestations. In other words, the stronger the manifestation, the more people expected the prophetic word to be powerful. Since not everyone had a Bible of their own in those days, ignorance of the Word accompanied with strong manifestations had disastrous consequences. There is no indication that the prophecies were judged, except by how strong the manifestations were when they occurred. In addition, the Huguenots were intensely persecuted, and the combined effect of prophets without teachers and extreme suffering produced a recipe for disaster. They had an undeniable experience, but the pain of seeing their friends and families slaughtered began to affect how they saw the world.

It is my personal opinion that the prophets became wounded in their spirits, which is why at the end they began to prophesy that the people should take up arms against their aggressors. The French prophets even prophesied that they would win in armed conflict, even though they were severely outnumbered. They went to war and were slaughtered by the thousands, until virtually nothing remained of their movement. They were taken out by the sword.

The Huguenots are an example of a dangerous tendency within prophetic movements that I have seen manifest more than once. History shows that the exaltation of prophecy, independent of the other spiritual gifts of teaching, pastoring, leadership, etc., invariably produces chaos. Because prophecy with manifestations is so powerful, people begin to consult prophets like oracles, and they stop listening to hear the voice of God themselves. Then they blindly obey what the prophets say and in so doing become spiritually blind. I am always nervous of prophets and prophetic words that encourage separation from the Body of Christ, claiming that the Lord "is calling for it" or "doing a new thing." Often the Lord has nothing to do with it. It might be that the prophet's wounding and rejection issues are at the root of such words. Prophets prophesy only "in part," and the ultimate goal of prophets is to equip a generation to bring about "the unity of the faith" and the "knowledge of the Son of God" (see Ephesians 4:13).

Revival Phenomena

In the next few pages, I will highlight the historical ecstatic phenomena of revival. Although there is not a direct correlation between such phenomena and ecstatic prophecy, there are definite similarities.

The Revival in England: John Wesley (1703–91)

Probably the most well known of all revival preachers is John Wesley, a brilliant Oxford fellow and lecturer who was converted at 35 and founded the Methodist movement. He traveled over 250,000 miles on horseback, preached over 40,000 sermons and wrote 5,000 sermons, tracts and pamphlets. John's brother, Charles, a partner in the work, wrote over 65,000 hymns! God used the two of them to transform the English world in their lifetimes. John Wesley experienced all the same phenomena in his meetings that are taking place today.

In April 1739, Wesley preached at Newgate Prison in Bristol. He recorded what happened as he preached:

> One, and another, and another sunk to the earth: They dropped on every side as thunderstruck. One of them cried aloud. We besought God on her behalf, and He turned her heaviness into joy. A second being in the same agony, we called upon God for her also; and He spoke peace unto her soul.[13]

The next day a doctor who suspected trickery or fraud accompanied Wesley to the prison to see for himself. Wesley describes how this doctor closely observed a woman:

[She] broke out into strong cries and tears. He went and stood close to her, and observed every symptom, 'til great drops of sweat ran down her face and all her bones shook. He then knew not what to think, being clearly convinced it was not fraud, nor yet any natural disorder. But when both soul and body were healed in a moment, he acknowledged the finger of God.[14]

Wesley went on to say:

When I began to pray, the flame broke out. Many cried aloud, many sank to the ground, many trembled exceedingly.[15]

Throughout his life Wesley witnessed such incredible revival phenomena that even though it was his preaching that God used, he himself was continually amazed. In one entry in his journal (July 29, 1759), Wesley recorded a number of examples that occurred while preaching:

Several fell to the ground, some of whom seemed dead, others in the agonies of death, the violence of their bodily convulsions exceeding all description. . . . A child, seven years old, sees many visions and astonishes the neighbors with her innocent awful manner of declaring them.[16]

Describing the same meeting Wesley details how the power of God now moved out into the churchyard. The people were affected in ways beyond what he could describe. One man was "wounded by the Lord." Wesley describes how he looked when others tried to hold him up:

His own shaking exceeded that of a cloth in the wind. It seemed as if the Lord came upon him like a giant, taking him by the neck and shaking all his bones in pieces. . . .
Another roared and screamed. . . .
Some continued long as if they were dead, but with a calm sweetness in their looks. I saw one who lay two or three hours in the open air, and, being then carried into the house,

continued insensible another hour, as if actually dead. The first sign of life she showed was a rapture of praise intermixed with a small, joyous laughter.[17]

A week later Wesley wrote, "I have generally observed more or less of these outward symptoms to attend the beginning of a general work of God. So it was in New England, Scotland, Holland, Ireland and many parts of England."[18]

The Revivals in America

Jonathan Edwards, New England Theologian-Pastor (1703–1758)

Seminary professor Richard Lovelace believes that "Jonathan Edwards may well be the greatest theologian and philosopher—and perhaps also the greatest mind—that America has yet produced."[19] Edwards first experienced manifestations of the Holy Spirit and became the chief spokesperson for revival while trying to bridge the difficult chasm between emotional excess and freedom of the Spirit. Edwards's own wife, Sarah, a mother of eleven children, experienced her own major visitation from God as she was incapacitated for seventeen days. Mr. Edwards supported and blessed the graces of God in both his wife and others:

[1740] It was a very frequent thing to see a house full of out-cries, faintings, convulsions and such like, both with distress, and also with admiration and joy. It was not the manner here to hold meetings all night, as in some places, nor was it common to continue them 'til very late in the night; but it was pretty often so, that there were some that were so affected, and their bodies so overcome, that they could not go home, but were obliged to stay all night where they were . . . and there were some instances of persons lying in a sort of trance, remaining perhaps for a whole 24 hours motionless, and with their senses locked up; but in the meantime under strong imaginations, as though they went to heaven and had there a vision of glorious and delightful objects. But when the people were raised to this height, Satan took the advantage, and his interposition, in many instances, soon became very apparent: and a great deal of caution and pains were found necessary to keep the people, many of them, from running wild.[20]

George Whitefield, English Methodist Revivalist (1714–1770)

George Whitefield was a contemporary of Wesley and Edwards and a personal friend of Benjamin Franklin. He preached at least eighteen thousand times to perhaps ten million hearers and also witnessed the same phenomena and manifestations of revival. Wesley at first chided Whitefield for not stopping the outward symptoms that were breaking out in his meetings. Later Wesley discovered that the symptoms were from God and not to be stopped. The accounts of Whitefield are detailed in his journals and are similar to those described by Wesley and Edwards.

Camp Meeting with Barton Stone at Cane Ridge, Kentucky (1801)

The following account is by the Rev. Moses Hodge, who witnessed the Cane Ridge meeting:

> The careless fall down, cry out, tremble and not infrequently are affected with convulsive twitchings. . . . Nothing that imagination can paint can make a stronger impression upon the mind than one of those scenes. Sinners dropping down on every hand, shrieking, groaning, crying for mercy, convulsed; professors praying, agonizing, fainting, falling down in distress, for sinners or in raptures of joy![21]

The following account is by James B. Finley, who witnessed the same meeting:

The noise was like a roar of Niagara. The vast sea of human beings seemed to be agitated as if by a storm . . . some of the people were singing, others praying, some crying for mercy in the most piteous accents, while others were shouting most vociferously. While witnessing these scenes, a peculiarly strange sensation such as I had never felt before came over me. My heart beat tumultuously, my knees trembled, my lips quivered and I felt as though I must fall to the ground. A strange supernatural power seemed to pervade the entire mass of mind there collected. . . . I stepped up on a log where I could have a better view of the surging sea of humanity. The scene that then presented itself to my mind was indescribable. At one time I saw at least five hundred swept down in a moment as if a battery of a thousand guns had been opened upon them and then immediately followed by shrieks and shouts that rent the very heavens.[22]

Peter Cartwright, Methodist Frontier Circuit-Rider (1785–1872)

The following is his account of "the jerks" at an early Kentucky camp meeting:

No matter whether they were saints or sinners, they would be taken under a warm song or sermon and seized with a convulsive jerking all over, which they could not by any possibility avoid, and the more they resisted the more they jerked. If they would not strive against it and pray in good earnest, the jerking would usually abate . . . To see these proud young gentlemen and young ladies, dressed in their silks, jewelry and prunella, from top to toe, take the jerks, would often excite my laughter. The first jerk or so, you would see their fine bonnets, caps and combs fly; and so sudden would be the jerking of the head that their long loose hair would crack almost as loud as a wagoner's whip.[23]

Charles Finney: The Revivals at Evan's Mills and DeKalb, New York (1825)

Charles Grandison Finney is considered America's greatest past revivalist. He is often credited with directly or indirectly being the instrument to bring about five hundred thousand conversions from 1825 to 1875.[24] Finney also witnessed phenomena, and in his own memoirs describes a personal experience where he "literally bellowed out the unutterable gushings" of his heart, as he was (what he calls) "baptized in the Spirit." Richard Riss says of this experience:

> He was in all probability describing what John Wesley described in several places as "roaring" at his meetings. . . . It is also of interest that, when one of the elders of his church arrived, the power of the Spirit came on him in the form of spasmodic laugher. It seemed as if it was impossible for him to keep from laughing from the very bottom of his heart.[25]

And the following revival account describes the phenomena of speechlessness:

> As the people withdrew I observed a woman in one part of the house being supported in the arms of some of her friends, and I went to see what was the matter, supposing that she was in a fainting spell. I soon found out that she was not fainting but that she could not speak. . . . I advised the women to take her home and pray with her to see what the Lord would do. They informed me that she was Miss G—, sister of the well-known missionary, and that she was a member of the church in good standing. . . . After lying in a speechless state about sixteen hours, Miss G—'s mouth was opened, and a new song was given her. She was taken from the horrible pit of miry clay, her feet were set upon a rock, and many saw it and feared.[26]

Frank Bartleman and the Azusa Street Revival (1907)

The following is an eyewitness account by this journalist at the Azusa Street, Los Angeles, visitation, which gave birth to the modern Pentecostal movement:

> Someone might be speaking. Suddenly the Spirit would fall upon the congregation. God himself would give an altar call. Men would fall all over the house, like the slain in battle, or

118

rush for the altar en masse, to seek God. The scene often resembled a forest of fallen trees. Such a scene cannot be imitated. . . . The whole place was steeped in prayer. God was in His holy Temple. It was for man to keep silent. The shekinah glory rested there.[27]

The accounts of the Azusa Street revival contain descriptions of every kind of phenomenon, including shaking, speechlessness, motionlessness, being enraptured, drunk in the Spirit, holy laughter, visions, tongues, prophecy and the like. I am sure that exaggerated examples can be found for each phenomenon, but to deny the countless testimonies of the overall authentic move of the Holy Spirit in the light of historical observation is to deny the most potent spiritual force to propel the Church in the twentieth century.

Present Day Revival

Right up to this present day, ecstatic prophecy in revival can be observed. The revival at the Brownsville Church in Pensacola, Florida, for example, was catalyzed by a shaking, ecstatic prophecy by a young woman. In the months of prayer that preceded this revival, the senior pastor of the church in which it occurred, John Kilpatrick, said he often was overcome by uncontrolled sobbing and shaking during prayer times, and at other times during the week he would feel a strange sensation in his stomach. He attributed these feelings to the Spirit of God coming upon him, preparing to manifest Himself to Brownsville.

The Coming Great Revival

Ecstatic prophecy is biblical, and it is historical. Over and over again, century after century, countless testimonies of ecstasy and ecstatic prophecy within authentic moves of the Spirit have been documented. In light of historical observation and in light of the known ways of God, we must acknowledge that ecstasy, or Holy Spirit possession, will likely occur in the coming great revival.

As we anticipate this coming revival, we cannot help but acknowledge that prophets and prophecy, especially ecstatic prophecy, almost seem to invite troubles and difficulties. After reading about the history of prophetic movements, with the strange behavior and the potential for division and misunderstanding, we might ask ourselves, *Why bother with something that has such latent possibility to become wildfire?*

The answer is that we are commanded in Scripture to desire, and not despise, prophecy (see 1 Corinthians 14:1; 1 Thessalonians 5:20). The knowledge of God is hidden not only in what He says through His prophets, but also in how He communicates to them. Eternal attributes are communicated not only through the words, but also through the modes of communication. God is not limited to what He has done before, but His nature is revealed through His actions. Even the mode or form of prophetic delivery, then, teaches us about the ways of God (see 1 Corinthians 1:25–27).

As believers, we never know how God will pour out His Spirit—whether softly or forcefully, strangely or commonly. But we can determine how we will respond when He does pour out His Spirit. Will we welcome the Spirit of prophecy, or will we reject it based upon what it looks like?

The natural Promised Land God chose for His children was full of giants. Similarly, promises of God that come through prophetic utterance also often come with giant obstacles and stumbling blocks. Church history has proven that giants dwell in the field where prophecy grows. But in the same field, promises, miracles and the knowledge of God also flourish. As we stand on the threshold of the coming great revival, I believe that it is worth enduring the troubles to find the treasure.

PART 2

JUDGING AND APPLYING ECSTATIC PROPHECY

8

DISCERNING THE SPIRITUAL SOURCE

We have now looked at ecstasy from many perspectives and discovered that adherents to most religions claim to have had some form of ecstatic prophetic experience, at least at certain points in history. The physical manifestations of the ecstatic experiences of different religions are startlingly similar. Both true prophets of God and false prophets have exhibited trancelike behavior or various levels of physical manifestations, ranging from trembling to seizures. So to outsiders, the prophetic behavior of different religions may look quite the same. There is, however, a major difference between the true and the false prophets, and the difference is the spiritual source of their prophecies. The source is either divine or demonic. For the Christian, the latter must be eschewed and the former embraced.

In the description of the book entitled *Discerning Spirits: Divine and Demonic Possession in the Middle Ages*, Nancy Caciola makes an important point as to the pervasiveness of the phenomenon and the lack of visible distinction between divine and demonic possession.

[Caciola] shows how medieval people decided whom to venerate as a saint infused with the Spirit of God and whom to avoid as a demoniac possessed of an unclean spirit. *Trance states, prophesying, convulsions, fasting and other physical manifestations were often regarded as signs that a person was seized by spirits*. . . . The discernment of spirits was central to the religious culture of Western Europe between 1200 and 1500. *Since the outward manifestations of benign and malign possession were indistinguishable*, a highly ambiguous set of bodily features and behaviors were carefully scrutinized by observers.[1]

Biblical Foundations for the Spiritual World

The Bible clearly teaches that the spiritual world does exist. Demonic spirits have power and often display it—as does the Holy Spirit. The God of the Bible is a God of incredible power, and He likes to make Himself known through these displays of power. Power encounters and/or signs are given to bring revelation of the one true God and to produce converts. Early on in the biblical narrative, we see the clash between people under the control of God's Spirit versus those controlled by demon spirits. Moses and the magicians of Pharaoh, for example, have one such power encounter (circa 1450 B.C.):

> So Moses and Aaron came to Pharaoh, and thus they did just as the LORD had commanded; and Aaron threw his staff down before Pharaoh and his servants, and it became a serpent. Then Pharaoh also called for the wise men and the sorcerers, and they also, the magicians of Egypt, *did the same* with their secret arts. For each one threw down his staff and they turned into serpents. But Aaron's staff swallowed up their staffs.
>
> Exodus 7:10–12, emphasis mine

> But the magicians of Egypt *did the same* with their secret arts; and Pharaoh's heart was hardened, and he did not listen to them, as the LORD had said.
>
> Exodus 7:22, emphasis mine

The magicians *did the same* with their secret arts, making frogs come up on the land of Egypt.

Exodus 8:7, emphasis mine

The sorcerers had spiritual power and were able to imitate the power of God up to a certain point. Apparently the Egyptians held widespread belief in the power of demonic sources—so much so that even Pharaoh had sorcerers in his court and at his disposal. They were able to channel the power of demons with dramatic results. But greater was the power of Moses' God than that of the sorcerers! When believers are confident in the greater power of our God, we will not run in fear when demons display their power. Instead we let our staff swallow up their staffs!

Another biblical account of an impressive spiritual power encounter occurred six hundred years later. This time the setting was not Egypt but Israel—Mount Carmel, to be exact. The prophets of Baal were facing down the great prophet Elijah. Though they tried to induce ecstasy by every means available (even cutting themselves), the demonic deity Baal could not hold a candle to God's display of power through His servant Elijah, and Elijah subsequently killed them all (see 1 Kings 18).

In the New Testament, too, we see power in demonic sources, as well as power from the Holy Spirit. The Gadarene demoniac (see Luke 8:26), for example, was possessed by demonic spirits. And in Acts 2, when the Holy Spirit was poured out, the early Church was possessed by the Holy Spirit. In Acts 8, the distinction between the two sources is quite evident:

> Now for some time a man named Simon had practiced sorcery in the city and amazed all the people of Samaria. He boasted that he was someone great, and all the people, both high and low, gave him their attention and exclaimed, "This man is the divine power known as the Great Power." They followed him because he had amazed them for a long time

125

with his magic. . . . And [Simon] followed Philip everywhere, astonished by the great signs and miracles he saw. Then Peter and John placed their hands on them, and they received the Holy Spirit. When Simon saw that the Spirit was given at the laying on of the apostles' hands, he offered them money and said, "Give me also this ability so that everyone on whom I lay my hands may receive the Holy Spirit."

Acts 8:9–11, 13, 17–19, NIV

Both Simon the sorcerer and the Christian apostles had power. But the greater power belongs to those who follow Jesus.

Since both the Old and New Testaments regularly attest to the power of both divine and demonic sources, the issue of source is the critical issue to consider, particularly when it comes to the subject of ecstatic prophecy. We are called repeatedly to test the source of spiritual power.

Test the Spirits

God's Word gives Christians a clear injunction to test spirits and make distinctions between false and true prophets:

> Beloved, do not believe every spirit, but test the spirits to see whether they are from God, because many false prophets have gone out into the world.

1 John 4:1

> Then the LORD said to me, "The prophets are prophesying falsehood in My name. I have neither sent them nor commanded them nor spoken to them; they are prophesying to you a false vision, divination, futility and the deception of their own minds."

Jeremiah 14:14

> But false prophets also arose among the people, just as there will also be false teachers among you, who will

secretly introduce destructive heresies, even denying the Master who bought them, bringing swift destruction upon themselves.

2 Peter 2:1

Therefore, thus says the Lord, "If you return, then I will restore you—before Me you will stand; and if you extract the precious from the worthless, you will become My spokesman."

Jeremiah 15:19

But examine everything carefully; hold fast to that which is good.

1 Thessalonians 5:21

As a safeguard against false prophets, God through His Holy Spirit also gives a distinct gift of discernment of spirits (see 1 Corinthians 12:10). We are to use God's Word and the gift of discernment to determine whether a manifestation is true or false.

For centuries believers have been trying to discern what is of God and what is of the devil. Even today accusations of "false prophets," "demon-possessed" people and "New Age" influence are bantered about continually. But what does it mean to test the spirits (see 1 John 4:1–3; 1 Corinthians 12:1–3)? The testing of spirits described in the Bible has nothing to do with what a manifestation looks like or whether someone missed a prophecy or prayed for someone who was not healed. It does not depend on how one feels or on whether or not something happens that may or may not have a biblical precedent. Rather, it has everything to do with doctrine and its resulting practice!

Testing the spirits is a complex procedure. No single test provides the complete measurement for prophetic veracity or reveals who is an authentic biblical prophet. Manifestations alone do not prove either divine or demonic source. Rather, the three points of the level are:

1. biblical orthodoxy (what one believes),
2. biblical behavior (how one lives) and
3. biblical content (the accuracy of the prophecy itself).[2]

The alignment of these three criteria should produce spiritual fruit.

Biblical Orthodoxy: What One Believes

This first test is easy, but only for those who know their Bibles well. All prophecy must align with the intent of the whole of the Bible. Any prophecy that is contrary to Scripture in any way is therefore to be totally and completely disregarded, no matter how it was delivered or who delivered it. If it came from an "angel," for example, or was accompanied by an extraordinary sign or miracle but does not align with biblical teaching, then it is false prophecy (see Galatians 1:8). If it is contrary to the Bible and leads the hearer away from God, then it cannot be from the God of the Bible.

"Be diligent to present yourself approved to God as a workman who does not need to be ashamed, accurately handling the word of truth" (2 Timothy 2:15). Prophets must know their Bibles well because most cults began with a mixture of biblical truth and false teaching. The Bible is often "added to" or "taken from," thus leaving an aberration of the truth.

The biblical injunction to test the spirits was given by the apostle John in order to help Christians really know "that He lives in us" and that the Spirit inspiring the message is from God. He writes:

And this is his command: to *believe* in the name of his Son, Jesus Christ, and to love one another as he commanded us. Those who obey his commands live in him, and he in them. And this is how we know that he lives in us: We know it by the Spirit he gave us.

1 John 3:23–24, NIV, emphasis mine

The context is orthodox Christianity. John says we can know that God lives in us by what we believe concerning the person of His Son, Jesus Christ.

Note what else John says:

> Dear friends, do not believe every spirit, but test the spirits to see whether they are from God, because many false prophets have gone out into the world. This is how you can recognize the Spirit of God: Every spirit that acknowledges that Jesus Christ has come in the flesh is from God, but every spirit that does not acknowledge Jesus is not from God. This is the spirit of the antichrist, which you have heard is coming and even now is already in the world. . . . They are from the world and therefore speak from the viewpoint of the world, and the world listens to them. We are from God, and whoever knows God listens to us; but whoever is not from God does not listen to us. This is how we recognize the Spirit of truth and the spirit of falsehood.
>
> 1 John 4:1–3, 5–6, NIV

John says that the test of spirits is what they say of Christ. Obviously more is meant than a superficial affirmation that "Jesus Christ has come in the flesh." It is all that this implies, as we see in Peter's great confession: "You are the Christ, the Son of the living God" (Matthew 16:16, NIV). The rock of Peter's confession was that this man Jesus was the Christ, the anointed One, the Messiah, the long-awaited Representative of God. To affirm that "Jesus Christ has come in the flesh" is not a trite verbal jingle. It is acknowledging an entire belief system.

Paul's entire treatise on spiritual gifts and the manifestations of the Spirit begins with the christological test. Paul writes to the Corinthian believers, "You know that when you were pagans, somehow or other you were influenced and led astray to mute idols" (1 Corinthians 12:2, NIV). It is a well-known fact that before they knew Christ they participated in pagan religions or cults, and their tongues, prophecy and miracles were performed by the power of demons (see 1 Corinthians 10:20).[3] Like John, Paul offers a test of the source and message of the spirit behind the gifts and manifestations the Corinthians were experiencing: "Therefore I tell you that no one who is speaking by the Spirit of God says, 'Jesus be cursed,' and no one can say, 'Jesus is Lord,' except by the Holy Spirit" (1 Corinthians 12:3, NIV). Again the test of the spirits was christology; that is, what do you confess about Christ? Those who confess an orthodox "Jesus is Lord" faith do so by the impetus of the Holy Spirit. The revelations and manifestations from people such as Joseph Smith, Mother Ann Lee or Muhammad can be measured and tested by their source: What do they say about Christ?

It is not about the strangeness of manifestations or the mishandling of gifts, even though the Bible does describe strange manifestations and does lay out guidelines for gifts used improperly. No, a false prophet or a false teacher is measured by what he or she confesses about the person of Jesus Christ—His Lordship, teaching and second coming. What is believed and confessed about Jesus is what determines which spirit has legal access to move in and produce a given work.

Biblical Behavior: How One Lives

But spiritual tests do not depend solely upon doctrine. They also are based upon practice.

Note that in the passage in 1 John mentioned above, the apostle also records a second part to God's command: to love one another as He commanded us (see 1 John 3:23). The command, therefore, is not simply what we believe but also how we behave. We are to obey His commandments and to love one another. The test to measure how we can be sure that we have the genuine article is first, *doctrine* and second, its spiritual outworking of fruit—*behavior.* Those who confess an orthodox "Jesus is Lord" faith must back up that confession with the life that Lordship demands.

One of the earliest extant Christian documents, *The Shepherd of Hermes*, a very early book (circa 95–100 A.D.) that was regarded as canonical by several early Church fathers,[4] gives some of the first instruction on how to discern false prophets from true prophets. Its main thesis is that true and false prophets primarily differ in their character. Both may know prophetic mysteries and knowledge, but the true prophet displays the character of Jesus.

> On the basis of what I am going to tell you, you can test the prophet from the false prophet. Determine the man who has the divine spirit by his life. . . . [He] is gentle and quiet and humble, and stays away from all evil and futile desires of this age, and considers himself to be poorer than others, and gives no answer to anyone when consulted. Nor does he speak on his own . . . but speaks when God wants him to speak.[5]

In other words, the fruit of the Spirit (gentleness, meekness, self-control, etc.) are apparent in the true prophet's life. As we test the spirits we must ask ourselves: What fruit results from the life of the prophet? Does his or her life produce spiritual fruit that comes from the Holy Spirit? "A good tree cannot bear bad fruit, and a bad tree cannot bear good fruit . . . Thus, by their fruit you will recognize them (Matthew 7:18, 20, NIV). It is my firm conviction that when real Christians seeking to build God's Kingdom are exhibiting truly spiritual fruit, critics of prophetic ecstasy have no biblical leg on which to stand.

In order to determine which prophecies have credence, one needs to examine the character and motivation of the prophet who gave them. In addition, the prophecies he or she gives should produce character in the lives of those who receive them. Godly character expressed through tangible service and righteous lifestyles always distinguishes true prophets from false ones.

Biblical Content: The Accuracy of the Prophecy Itself

Testing or judging prophecy is not rocket science. For the most part, it is an easy thing to do. Basically, there are four possibilities when it comes to judging prophecy:

1. The prophecy is true.
2. The prophecy is speaking to one's potential (future truth).
3. The prophecy is right but wrong (a mixture).
4. The prophecy is false.

Let's look at these four possibilities in more detail.

1. The prophecy is true.

How do we know that a prophecy is true? A personal prophecy will first witness to both your spirit and your reality. Details in the prophecy will be measurable and clear and will confirm a direction in which the Lord has been leading you. The prophecy may be edification, exhortation or comfort—perhaps God is simply letting you know He loves you, knows you and is for you. "If God is for us, who can be against us?" (Romans 8:31). Though the prophecy may be simple, it will give you courage and strength to move forward.

Second, the prophecy may contain such authority that it launches you into a new ministry direction. If the prophecy is very direct, however, do not quit your day job and move to another city. Just stay put. Wait for the prophecy to be confirmed "by the mouth of two or three" (Matthew 18:16). Pray for both natural and spiritual confirmation. Even if all the above happens, you then need the endorsement of important people in your life, such as parents (if you are living at home), pastors and spiritual mentors. A personal prophecy does not ever supersede the existing authority of clearly defined authority structures of family and church leadership. Take the time to pray and wait until the Lord brings alignment in these several key areas. This does not mean that things cannot unfold quickly—they might. But we want to do the Lord's work the Lord's way and follow the whole of the Bible, not one prophetic word.

If all of these things line up and the prophecy is in agreement with the teaching of Scripture, then the prophecy is a true one and from the Lord.

2. *The prophecy is speaking to one's potential (future truth).*

Sometimes we can tell immediately if a prophecy is true, and sometimes we cannot. Sometimes a prophecy indicates potential and is a kind of invitation from the Lord. God certainly has way more planned for all of us than we can imagine or are capable of. God sees us differently than we see ourselves.

The first prophetic word I received in our Baptist church was way over my head, way beyond my Plymouth Brethren theology. Somebody stood at the front of our church, picked me out of the crowd and said, "I see you standing in front of hundreds and thousands of people." At the time I had never even considered preaching, had never spoken in church and had no desire to do so. That prophecy was not fulfilled until ten years later. Ten years. But years later when I was speaking at a women's conference in Mexico with 23,000 women, I suddenly remembered that prophecy. I realized that I never made that prophecy come to pass—not at any level. I was just faithful in the little things God gave me to do, faithfully teaching the two-year-old class every week for five years.

Sometimes prophecies seem so far off that we simply reject them without even praying about them. Sometimes destiny is stopped through unbelief (see Hebrews 4). Judge your prophetic word. When you are unsure or when it seems impossible, give God your heart and say, "There is no way I can—or even want to—do this, but I give You the whole of my heart. I will do anything and go anywhere. God, if this prophecy is from You, then You have to work in my heart and circumstances to bring it about because right now it is impossible." God loves a submissive heart; it is precious in His sight (see 1 Peter 3:4).

I was called out of children's ministry into prophetic ministry through several prophetic words. Initially, when I received prophetic words saying I should leave children's ministry, it was really hard for me. I was not willing to hear those words. I loved children's ministry. So I disregarded the prophecies. Within a short period of time, however, many different people gave me the same prophetic word. So I asked for every prophecy to be written, and every night before I went to bed I would pray through those prophetic words and say, "God, if this is really You, then change my heart." After praying every night for over a month and talking it over with my husband, I decided God was asking me to change ministry direction. I laid down children's ministry and turned all of my ministry emphasis toward pursuing prophecy. Had I not received those directive words, I probably never would have done that. It took that month of prayer and testing the prophecies for my heart to catch up with what God had in store for me.

In short, you can receive a true prophecy, but it might not witness to you right away. Do not worry: If you are hard of hearing, God will keep telling you the same thing until you get it.

Prophecy can speak to the potential. God loves to speak to your potential. You might not feel adequate, but remember your "adequacy is from Him" (2 Corinthians 3:5).

3. The prophecy is right but wrong (a mixture).

In the New Testament, prophecy is not infallible. We therefore must weigh and test all prophecy, no matter who gives it.

When a prophet prays for others, he or she may be able to sense the person's desires, rather than God's desires, and the prophet can mistakenly mix them up when he/she is prophesying. I know a pastor who received a prophetic word from a well-known, respected prophet. The prophet told him, "You are going to be used mightily in God's Kingdom. You will evangelize and preach the Gospel like Billy Graham, but you will evangelize with signs and wonders." The leader who received the prophecy was initially very excited.

What the prophet did not know was that this pastor loved Billy Graham. He owned every book written by and about Billy Graham. Billy Graham was his spiritual hero. Out of all the men on earth, he looked up to Billy Graham the most. Since he was also a charismatic pastor, the idea of evangelizing with signs and wonders was absolutely exhilarating.

Seven years later, however, after planting churches and doing all sorts of other ministry but doing little evangelism and very few signs, this pastor became disillusioned. He realized that his primary gift was not evangelism but discipleship. At the end of seven years, the prophecy was kind of like a bitter pill.

What happened? The prophet was partially right: The pastor had done mighty things in the Kingdom of God. But the prophet also had picked up on the desires of the man's heart, rather than the desires of God's heart for that pastor. So the second part of the prophecy was not true.

When given a prophetic word, the receiver must ask, "Is this who God has made me? Is it potential? Can I get there?" Ask yourself if this is a desire solely of your heart, or if it is a desire of God's heart for you. Again, seek confirmation from two or three others. Test the prophecy against God's Word. Ask God to reveal His true desire for you. You, not the prophet, are responsible to weigh and test that word.

If you discover that the prophecy is right but wrong, then your attitude should be, "Well, praise the Lord, I surely do love that prophet. Even though he was wrong, he helped me define my calling." Prophets are doing the best they can, and they are not infallible. And remember that the prophecy can be right but completely wrongly interpreted or wrongly applied.

4. The prophecy is false.

I have heard of some real prophetic bloopers. Just the other day a senior pastor told me the following true story of a prophecy given in his church. It was a Sunday morning service, and thousands were in attendance. The worship came to a crescendo and was followed by a pungent silence. Suddenly a woman stood up and declared, "I am the Holy Spirit—and I am not here!" Whoops! That was easy to judge.

Laughing, the same pastor told me of another prophecy he heard with his own ears: "Behold, I am the Lord God of Joshua, who said, 'Let My people go!' who crossed the Red Sea, who . . ." The "prophet" went on and on to describe a long list of the acts that "the Lord God of Joshua" did, when the acts were clearly things that Moses did. Finally the "prophet" sat down, and all was silent. Several minutes later the "prophet" stood up again and declared, "Behold, the Lord your God maketh a mistake." Whoops again!

Yes, false prophets do exist. Sometimes false prophecy is intentional. Sometimes people are self-seeking and try to puff themselves up. They place their need to be noticed above God's truth. Their own needs supersede the needs of the Body. This is why it is so important to test each prophecy.

Most of the time, however, an incorrect prophecy is a mistake. Prophets are sinful human beings; they make mistakes. But I am glad we are New Testament prophets. We can have bad days, miss the mark and not be stoned on account of it. If we miss it, we must be humble enough to apologize: "I was wrong. I am sorry." We should never blame the mistake on God (i.e., "The Lord your God maketh a mistake") when the prophecy came out of the flesh. We must simply be humble and admit when we are wrong.

In the New Testament, God gives many different gifts. A person may have the gift of preaching but have a bad day and give a lousy sermon. We do not throw out the whole gift because of one day. Or a person may have a gift of healing and might pray for a person who gets worse. This one experience does not negate the person's gift.

I try to persuade the Church to have a little more grace toward prophets because we are doing the best we can. Every time we prophesy, it takes faith. If others will do their job of weighing and testing prophecy, then it makes the prophet's job of prophesying according to his/her faith a bit easier.

One time I experienced something awful. I prayed for a pregnant mother. About a month later a close friend of the woman called to tell me that this woman had suffered a miscarriage. Her words were urgent: "Stacey, you have got to phone this couple because you prayed for them, and you said things that were not true." I was just sick because the baby had died. I immediately called the couple. I gave them my condolences and then asked for their forgiveness. "If I in any way hurt you, I want to apologize. If anything I said was wrong, I take responsibility for that. I am really sorry, and I want you to know I am praying for you." The father was crying on the other end of the phone. Through tears he said, "Thank you so much for phoning. Actually, I took the tape out today and listened to the prophecy you spoke over us. When I listened to the prophecy again, I discovered that I had interpreted things certain ways. You actually never said what I thought you did. It was really clean and really good." I was relieved about that, but what was so meaningful to me was that he said, "Thank you so much for phoning." And when that couple eventually did have a baby a few years later, he made sure that I knew about it.

But for a while I was spooked by that experience. *Wow,* I thought, *People take every word I say to heart. What if I say something wrong?* It made me afraid to prophesy. I took it to the Lord in prayer, and eventually I realized that my responsibility was to prophesy according to my faith. None of us is infallible; we will make mistakes. And when we do, we have to take responsibility for those mistakes and seek healing.

Who Tests Prophecy?

New Testament prophets are different from Old Testament prophets. New Testament prophecy is to be judged; it is for edification, exhortation and comfort. It is not Scripture; therefore, prophets no longer need to be stoned when they are wrong. The New Testament has a safety net: All prophecies should be weighed carefully, then judged, and the parts that are good and precious should be extracted from the worthless. "Do not quench the Spirit; do not despise prophetic utterances. But examine everything carefully; hold fast to that which is good" (1 Thessalonians 5:19–21).

Biblically, it is not the prophet's responsibility to judge his or her own prophecies. Scripture indicates that the prophet is merely the messenger (see Ezekiel 33:2–9). Revelation is to be tested by the individual or group to whom the prophecy is given. "Weigh carefully what is said" (1 Corinthians 14:29, NIV). In other words, if a person receives a personal prophecy, that person is responsible to weigh it himself, and/or to seek counsel on the prophecy. If a prophecy is given to a church, then it becomes the responsibility of the leadership of that church to weigh the word. Again, this is not the prophet's responsibility. So when a prophet misses a word, the responsibility to follow up on it must be initiated by the leadership. The prophet may need to publicly acknowledge missing it, but the greater responsibility lies with the leadership, who must steward and pastor the prophecy (and the prophet) in the context in which it was given.

Determine What Is Real

It has been said, "All that glitters is not gold." And yet gold exists. This saying is not meant to encourage us to throw away everything that looks like gold; if we did that, we might throw out some real gold in the process. On the contrary, we must use the science available to us to determine what is real gold and what is "fool's gold." In the same way, the Bible talks about real prophets and false prophets. Both exist. And the Bible calls us to use discernment and judge prophecy by using measurable and clear biblical tests. The crux of the issue is whether the source of each individual prophetic experience is God or the devil.

9

PROPHETS AND CHARACTER

In the last chapter we talked briefly about the behavior of the prophet being one test for discerning the spiritual source. Of course, we Christians are at various levels of maturity, and all of us have room for improvement. It is important, however, for all of us—and especially prophets, because of the inherent power of spiritual knowledge—to exhibit an interior desire for holiness, humility and honor for the Body of Christ. Let us therefore look a little more in depth at the issue of prophets and character.

Prophets Must Abide in the Vine

Spiritual fruit is produced by abiding in the vine, not by working harder. It comes from a deep relationship with Jesus, and such fruit brings Him glory (see John 15:2, 4, 5, 8). This is a significant point, especially for prophets. Godliness is a byproduct of relationship with God.

It is, therefore, a serious deception for prophets to have revelation *from* God when there is no relationship *with* God.

It is a scary thing, but it is actually possible to believe that we are hearing from God without knowing Him. And revelation apart from relationship is nothing more than deception.

> Not everyone who says to Me, "Lord, Lord," will enter the kingdom of heaven, but he who does the will of My Father who is in heaven will enter. Many will say to Me on that day, "Lord, Lord, did we not prophesy in Your name, and in Your name cast out demons, and in Your name perform many miracles?" And then I will declare to them, "I never knew you; depart from me, you who practice lawlessness."
>
> Matthew 7:21–23

Deception results when a person has spiritual power or spiritual knowledge but no desire to know the Giver of the power or the knowledge. When false beliefs are "substantiated" by real prophetic revelation or demonstrations of power, many can be deceived. The Bible calls this sorcery (see Acts 8:9). This is one of the great dangers at the end of the age. Paul specifically warned us that delusion given through deceivers with lying signs and wonders would be a reality (see 2 Thessalonians 2:1–11).

In order to avoid practicing sorcery, then, the prophet must abide in the vine, knowing his Lord intimately. Fruit comes from abiding in the vine, from leaning on our Beloved, from intimacy with Jesus. Only true intimacy with Jesus (see John 15:5) will protect us from the seducing power of false intimacy.

Prophets and Pride

When a prophet has great spiritual knowledge, pride can also set in easily, and pride is subtle. Since prophecy is a gift with which to serve others, to build them up and to comfort them (see 1 Corinthians 14:3), pride and prophecy should be mutually exclusive.

In addition, prophecy is "the testimony of Jesus," and He is the most humble person who ever lived. Therefore, a gift testifying of Him should be accompanied with mega humility (see Philippians 2:1–8).

Sadly, however, pride and prophecy do coexist. And pride can open prophets to deception and seduce them into all kinds of false beliefs, giving foothold to the enemy of prophets, the Jezebel spirit, to further seduce them into immorality.

The spirit of Jezebel is a spiritual power that attacks God's bondservants (see Revelation 2:20, 22). The Bible talks about spiritual "powers" (Ephesians 6) that fight against humans. Often these spiritual powers have names (i.e., Apollyon in Revelation 9:11 and Beelzebub in Matthew 12:27 and Mark 3:22), and sometimes these names depict what they do or whom they represent. The common name behind the spiritual power assigned particularly to prophets is the Jezebel spirit.

This name comes from a real woman named Jezebel, who seduced many of the Israelite prophets under her authority (see 1 Kings 18:4, 13), thereby neutralizing their gift and stripping them of their power. Today the spirit of Jezebel's primary mandate is to seduce and subdue prophets/bondservants—to get them under her influence (see 2 Kings 9:30; Revelation 2:20).

I have observed that one of Jezebel's great seductions is to cause prophets to focus on revelation apart from relationship. Prophetic knowledge without love makes us nothing in the sight of God (see 1 Corinthians 13:2). Knowledge breeds arrogance, instead of edification (see 1 Corinthians 8:1). It is a spiritual principle that pride comes before destruction (see Proverbs 16:18). We must, therefore, make it a lifestyle as prophets to focus on Jesus, not prophecy, in order to be protected from such destruction.

Holiness

The only way we overcome Jezebel is by abiding in the vine and continually washing ourselves in the blood of the Lamb. Practical holiness, or righteousness, is a fruit that comes from abiding in the vine. We cannot be righteous apart from the blood of Jesus. But how do we take these spiritual concepts and make them practical in daily life?

When I was a young Christian, I did not understand the concept of righteousness through the blood of Jesus. I mean, I understood it in my head, but practically I felt that if I were good, then God liked me, but if I were bad, then He would withdraw from me. Whenever I would sin or have a bad attitude, I would therefore either try to run from God or spend all my prayer time repenting. This worked for a while. I generally was able to be "pretty good," until one day when I suddenly developed an eating disorder. For the first time in my life I was no longer able to be "good." I entered an eight-month period of binging and purging, praying and repenting virtually daily. The harder I tried, the more addicted I became. I was so broken at the end of this period that I began to think that perhaps I was no longer saved—that I surely could not be a Christian since I could not be good. I was sinning daily and getting worse by the month. I hated myself for it, and I convinced myself that God did not like me because I was so bad.

One night I went to a Christian concert, and the singer was singing about the love of God. Since I was at the point where I thought God did not love me due to my daily, habitual sin, I could not connect at any level with what the singer was describing in his song. But when I looked up at the worship leader, I saw a vision of Jesus above his head. As I stared at Jesus, I felt wave after wave of unconditional love emanating from Him. I felt as if liquid waves of love were pouring through every cell of my being, and I began to weep profusely. I was shocked to feel this love that was so undeserved. But it was the most pure and overwhelming love I ever experienced. I was undone. I could feel this love, this undeserved pure and perfect love, all around and in and through me. It was so beautiful. After soaking me in His love for some time, Jesus audibly spoke to me, and I could not believe what He said. It was the last thing I thought He would say, considering my daily sinful behavior. He said, "If you do that until the day you die, *I will still love you.*" I wept and wept and wept. Before those words, I followed Jesus because He was the Truth. But the moment I heard those words, I fell in love with Jesus. He loves me. He loved me when I hated myself. Twenty-seven years later, I still weep when I think of those words, and I am overwhelmed with the grace of God. Nothing can separate us from the love of God, not even sin. Sin was paid for and washed away by the blood of God.

Of course, I still sin since I have not reached the state of sinless perfection. So I regularly take a blood bath, bringing myself before the cross, gazing at Jesus and worshiping Him for every drop of blood that He shed. I think about what He meant when He said, "It is finished" (John 19:30). It *is* finished. Every sin that separated me from God has been atoned. For me, taking a blood bath means meditating on what the shed blood of Jesus did to wash away every sin—past, present and future—and believing that nothing can ever separate me from the love of God—not even sin. I really do believe this, so now when I sin I run *to* God, and not *from* God. I turn even my sin to worship, and the practical result of this worship is that I sin less. I do not ever want to sin, but when I do, I know where and how to get rid of its sting. Sin does not have dominion over me because Jesus had dominion over sin, and I live in the grace of His victory (see Romans 6:14). I hide myself in God, and He strengthens me in my inner man.

We prophets must continually take "blood baths" in order to walk in holiness, rather than in habitual sin. Hidden sin pollutes the vessel. Since we are the temples of the Holy Spirit, we have to clean house regularly. Bad attitudes, sins of the flesh, unforgiveness—we must stay free of them. Without coming clean, we open ourselves up to deception, and sin affects our prophetic gift. We then prophesy out of a wrong spirit. We prophets have to keep a clean conscience before God first, and men second. Only when we stay clean can God use us to give holy words to His people.

Humility

The key to overcoming pride is humility. Once we are washed clean by our Savior's blood, we must clothe ourselves with humility.

Jesus is our standard for humility. Everything about Him is humble. As is evidenced by His birthplace (a stable), His poverty, His hiddenness ("Who do you say I am?") and His place of death (a cross), no one is more humble than God. Somehow the testimony of Jesus, the Spirit of prophecy, must reflect this important attribute of God's nature.

I have the privilege of going to a lot of prophetic conferences. Usually almost everyone wants me to prophesy over him or her. I used to resent this because it felt as if people were focusing on me instead of God. I got to the point where I just wanted to run off the stage after speaking and talk to no one. But one day I was reading the gospels and noticed Jesus' response to the clamoring crowds. I read about the woman with the issue of blood, the children who were brought to Jesus by their mothers, blind Bartimaeus, etc. In all of these stories, the disciples essentially said, "Don't bother the Teacher." But Jesus said, "Let them come to Me." He noticed who touched Him. He said, "Your faith has made you whole." I realized that Jesus loved people, even when they were grasping for something from Him. He saw beyond the desperation to the faith, and He stopped, blessed them and healed them. Humility, then, is sometimes expressed in service, and prophets serve by prophesying.

While I still sometimes find myself wanting to quit, hide and retreat when I am in a crowd with people pulling at me, I know now that Jesus rarely ran from people. Whether He was tired, hungry, facing His enemies or spending time with His friends, Jesus loved. "God so loved the world that He gave" (John 3:16). He said to me, *Stacey, prophecy is the gift I gave you so that you can give, too. What you do to them, you do to Me.* I was deeply struck by the following verses: John

13:34–35; 14:15, 21 (especially), 23; 15:9, 10, 12–14, 17. Jesus has taught me that I can love Him by how I love people. I do not have to be praying or singing to show my love for Him. I can be serving, and even turn my prophesying into an act of worship.

These verses made me wonder if perhaps one of the earthly indicators of how we are doing at obeying Commandment One is demonstrated by how we are doing at obeying Commandment Two, the "new commandment" He gave us. Jesus said, "If you keep my commandments, you will abide in my love. . . . This is My commandment, that you love one another just as I have loved you" (John 15:10, 12). Instead of feeling harassed by the crowds, I have learned to view them as a way to love and worship God.

Loving God's people shows humility in the prophet. The combination of the two, humility and love for others, are key behaviors that must be evident in the life of the true prophet.

Knowing When to Retreat

In prophetic ministry it is sometimes difficult to know when to go forward and when to retreat. But I do believe that it is essential to find the rhythm between the lonely place and the crowd.

Prophets prefer the lonely places (see Mark 1:45; Luke 5:16). It has taken a while, but I have learned to move somewhat freely between the crowds and the lonely places (having five children has definitely helped!). In certain ways, crowds can even be a deep place for loving Jesus—sometimes even deeper than solitude. However, extended times of "beholding God" through His Word are vital in maintaining intimacy with God. Part of mature prophetic character is knowing how and when to move into the prophetic anointing and when to retreat into the quiet, lonely place.

Honor for the Body of Christ

In serving the Body of Christ with the gift of prophecy for many years, I have noticed a disturbing trend in some prophetic communities. Because persecution is the plight of prophets, wounded prophets often separate from or turn against the Body of Christ.

In every family, issues arise, and this principle is just as true in the Body of Christ. But we are the Body of Christ. If one weeps, we all weep; if one rejoices, we all rejoice. First Peter 2:17 challenges us to "honor all people, love the brotherhood." We are all one family—one Body with the same Lord. All prophets must realize that we need to build up the Body, because it is our own Body. We are as much a part of the Body as anyone, and we must never destroy or hate our own, but rather "honor . . . and love the brotherhood."

Character Distinguishes the True from the False

There is no quick way to character. Character is produced decision by decision, day in and day out. Choosing lowliness and holiness are especially critical to the prophet. Godly character expressed through tangible service and righteous lifestyles are indicators that distinguish the true prophets from the false ones.

10

ECSTASY IN THE ASSEMBLY—HOW TO FUNCTION

God is big. Really big. His invisible attributes, eternal power and divine nature are evident in the greatness of creation (see Romans 1:19–20).

Creation often speaks to me about the creativity and diversity of God's nature. When my children were small, I took them to the Taronga Zoo in Sydney, Australia—one of the most amazing places I have ever visited because of its diversity of animal life. They have white snow leopards, komodo dragons, platypuses, white and orange Bengal tigers, wildebeests and so much more. I remember being in awe of God as I walked through that zoo with my kids. Every animal was different, every creature unique.

When I travel around the world and observe different cultures and see God's image in people of so many different skin types, worship styles and socioeconomic settings, I stand in awe of Him. I think God is so great that even if we put all the billions of people made in His image in one place at one time and then looked at the reflection of His image in all those gathered, we would still barely touch the surface of His creative genius and greatness.

This principle of biodiversity, through which God's divine nature and invisible attributes are clearly seen, has a lot of bearing on church gatherings. God gives gifts to His people, and the gifts are very different. In the natural world, when a bunch of different people from different cultures and strata of society with different worldviews gather together, the end result of their mutual encounter is not unity. People like to gather with like-minded people. They just feel better that way. They can understand and be understood. But God does not think like people. He loves diversity—many members, one Body. So when He gives gifts to men, He mixes everything up and puts all kinds of different people together, giving each of them different gifts with varying measures of anointing. The strange thing is that His expected outcome from such a scenario is the unity of the faith, the knowledge of the Son of God and maturity:

> And He gave some as apostles, and some as prophets, and some as evangelists, and some as pastors and teachers, for the equipping of the saints for the work of service, to the building up of the body of Christ; until we all attain to the unity of the faith, and of the knowledge of the Son of God, to a mature man, to the measure of the stature which belongs to the fullness of Christ.
>
> Ephesians 4:11–13

Who can know the mind of our Creator? How do we understand His ways? We need to learn the prayer of Moses: "If I have found favor in Your sight, then let me know Your ways that I may know You, that I may find favor in Your sight" (Exodus 33:13).

God's Brilliant Strategy

As I mentioned in the introduction to this book, I am married to a man with a completely different spiritual gift than mine. He functions apostolically. He loves to build the Kingdom. He loves to take new ground, feels most comfortable in big events with lots of people, sees the big picture and dreams about how to save the world. Although a few exceptions exist, I have noticed that most apostles are like my husband. God made them this way. God has gifted them with the desire to take care of the "99 sheep" (see Matthew 18:11–13).

Prophets, on the other hand, like to think about God. They prefer solitude to crowds, like the lonely places, think deep and not wide, obsess about certain things and are sensitive to issues that never cross an apostolic mind. They will not necessarily take care of any people because their main focus is God.

Pastors are different from both apostles and prophets. Their hearts are turned to people. They are shepherds. They will leave the 99 for the one lost sheep over and over again. They do not think in terms of crowds; they think in terms of individuals. They love God by doing to the least what they would do to Jesus.

Teachers are different from all of these. Like prophets, teachers are not as interested in people. They love the law of God and could spend all day sitting in a small room poring over the Word, not talking to one person. People are the backdrop to which the teacher teaches.

And finally, there are the evangelists. They love people—as long as those people are not in the Church. In other words, they sometimes get frustrated with Church people, but they sure love the lost. Their mantra is, *We gotta get out there and evangelize!*

Obviously these descriptions of the different gifts are generalizations, but inherent within different gifts are passions for different things. From God's big perspective, the strategy is brilliant. Everyone and everything gets taken care of: the 99, the one, the Spirit, the Word and the lost. Awesome! The whole world can come to God.

Attaining Unity

From man's small perspective, however, the diversity is extreme. The potential for division is high. Simply putting people with two different gifts in one room, say prophets and pastors, can cause shockwaves. Now if we add something as extreme as ecstatic prophecy to an already diverse group of people with divergent spiritual accents and worldviews, then the shockwaves below the surface can trigger a veritable tsunami of difficulties in a local church or ministry. In other words, if ecstatic prophecy is added to the equation, whole churches can implode.

Unrestrained excess of any of the above gifts—or any mixture of those gifts—can turn order into chaos. But if God gives these gifts and His stated goal for giving them is to bring about, among other things, "the unity of the faith," then surely there is a way to attain that unity. So how do we allow for the genuine, pastor the weak and those growing in varieties of gifts, not quench the Spirit but not blow up the local church?

The Church is a spiritual building, not a natural one. Although natural dynamics come into play and can be used to facilitate the advance of God's Kingdom, the primary way to build His Church is to use spiritual principles, the greatest of which is love. And love is hard. We are created for His pleasure, to love Him with everything we are. We are His, and He is ours. In every second of time and in every situation we find ourselves, we can receive His love and give love back to Him. As I shared earlier, one of the primary ways we give love back to Him is through the second commandment (see John 13:34; 14:15, 21, 23–24; 15:10, 12–13, 17). Unity, therefore, can be attained through love.

Although this is common knowledge for every Christian, it is not easy to do. It is possible to do, but not easy. Only by leaning on the wisdom of God and loving Him with our whole hearts can we bring about unity, the knowledge of God and maturity in the Body. But God likes us to lean. Leaning is good (see Song of Solomon 8:5; Proverbs 3:5).

In the Room: When and Where

Jesus said, "In my Father's house are many mansions" (John 14:2, KJV). God's house has a lot of different rooms. Nevertheless it is still one house. It takes a wise Master Builder to put all the living stones together in such a way that they do not cave in on each other.

Prophecy can have a room in the house, but prophecy is not the whole house. The same holds true for all the gifts. But I want now to focus our discussion on prophets. From what I have observed, one of the most effective ways to build prophets, ecstatic or otherwise, is to give them their own room.

Our home church was a prophetic one, with many different kinds of revelatory gifts from seer to ecstatic. Once our revival season was over, however, we did not often have prophetic words on Sunday mornings. We had a prophetic department that was open to anybody in the church who wanted to come, and we met on Monday nights. We had a service with a prophetic worship band, a prophetic teaching and an open prophetic time. People who had prophetic words could give them under the direction of the leader. Every type and stripe of prophecy was welcome—visions, dreams, prophetic singers, prophetic dancers, ecstatics, words of knowledge, dark sayings (see Numbers 12:8), prophetic intercessors—you name it, we allowed it as long as it was in submission to leadership. All the words were recorded, and once a month we gave a written summary of what the Lord was saying to our church elders. They weighed the summary, and upon their approval we put it in the Sunday morning bulletin. In addition, we had all kinds of prophetic cell groups—men's prophetic groups, women's prophetic groups, prophetic intercession meetings, values training cell groups, weekend prophetic conferences, prophetic worship groups, etc. I also regularly took prophetic teams with me to conferences where I was speaking. But it was not all that common for us to prophesy at the Sunday morning services. Sometimes it happened, but usually not. Usually we just published a monthly prophetic synopsis in the bulletin.

As we observed earlier, Paul addressed the issue of "when and where" in 1 Corinthians 14, where he talks about tongues. There is a time and a place for spiritual gifts. Of course, God does sometimes break in and do whatever He wants, but generally there is a time and a place to operate in the various spiritual gifts. When we operate in a spirit of honor, esteeming others better than ourselves, we will love to respect the directives of time and place.

This is a particularly important principle for ecstatic prophets to observe. By nature, ecstasy is demonstrative—therefore, distracting. If God is doing something personal with me in a corporate setting and I am the only one manifesting, I leave the room. Nobody else knows what is going on inside of me, and it takes them away from focusing on Jesus to focusing on me. I do not want that. When I am leading a meeting and this happens to others, I ask them to leave the room. Why? Don't I want the Spirit to move? Of course I do! But I want the Spirit to move on everybody, and I know He moves different ways with different people. I do not want to distract others from their worship experience because of one person's demonstrative ecstatic experience. If it is not appropriate for the corporate expression, then just as with tongues, it is better to do it at home (see 1 Corinthians 14:17, 19).

Love versus Freedom

Love is a higher principle than freedom. Paul restricted himself "for the sake of his brother" from allowable freedoms.

Knowledge makes arrogant, but love edifies. If anyone supposes that he knows anything, he has not yet known as he ought to know; but if anyone loves God, he is known by Him. Therefore concerning the eating of things sacrificed to idols, we know that there is no such thing as an idol in the world, and that there is no God but one. . . . However, not all men have this knowledge. . . . But take care that this liberty of yours does not somehow become a stumbling block to the weak. . . . For through your knowledge he who is weak is ruined, the brother for whose sake Christ died. And so, by sinning against the brethren and wounding their conscience when it is weak, you sin against Christ. Therefore, if food causes my brother to stumble, *I will never eat meat again*, so that I will not cause my brother to stumble.

1 Corinthians 8:1–4, 7, 9, 11–13, emphasis mine

Paul's attitude is so beautiful to me. He would never eat meat again if it caused his brother to stumble. If we apply the love versus freedom principle to ecstatic experiences or manifestations (like tongues in 1 Corinthians 14), then the highest principle of all is to love and honor and not offend.

I never need to prophesy where it will offend or trip up my brothers. Generally, this occurs inside the Church, not outside of it, so I choose love over freedom. I want the Church to be built up, not torn down or divided. I want to honor leaders and pastors who have different perspectives or theologies than mine. It is my goal to strengthen the Church, not weaken it. So I choose not to divide and never to quit. Anyone who knows me has often heard me say, "If you don't quit, you win." In other words, if people do not understand me or if they oppose me because of how I prophesy, I choose to honor them anyway, to love them anyway and not to end my relationship with them. As much as lies within me, I am to work at being at peace with all men (see Hebrews 12:14).

Besides, as I shared earlier, prophets tend to see deep and not wide, and sometimes we are unaware of the way the macrodynamics of a given setting are affected. It is not necessarily our gift. Many times I have been protected, and others have been protected, from unnecessary fallout, simply by choosing the higher principle of love over freedom. Love will work for the good of everyone. Once again, unity can be obtained through love.

Pastoring Prophets

But while the prophets have their responsibility to maintain unity in the Body, the Body has a responsibility to prophets as well. The prophets desperately need pastoring.

Pastoring prophetic people can be difficult, and the potential for problems is legion. Prophets often struggle with oversensitivity, with more gifting than character (see 1 Corinthians 13), with jealousy and quarrels, with wanting to be what they are not (see 1 Corinthians 12:14–30). Some feel God does not love them because they do not manifest, and others wonder why they are manifesting. Those who are trying to find their significance through the prophetic gift exude an offensive odor of ambition. At times the Church shuts down the prophetic person through criticism and judging. At other times the person with revelation so intensely feels the burden or warning of the prophecy that he or she internalizes the word and actually turns against the Body. All of these situations are messes, and we have not even gotten out the big shovels yet.

It takes an even larger shovel to scoop up the mess of wrong prophecies or nonprophecies. There are always those who think they are prophetic but are not. Then, as I said, there are those who mix true revelation with their own "stuff." And even worse situations develop when leaders weigh the prophetic word (see 1 Corinthians 14:29) and determine that the word is off, but the prophet will not receive the correction. Convinced that he or she has heard from God, the revelatory person will not lay it down.

Finally prophets and churches face problems of revelation, interpretation and application. Revelation is discerning what is seen or heard in the Spirit. Interpretation is determining what is meant by what is seen or heard. And application is understanding how to apply that which was seen or heard. A prophetic word or picture must be given and evaluated, then skillfully pastored into the life of a church or individual.

As you can see, potential minefields surround the prophetic gift in the Church. The proverb rings true: "Where no oxen are, the manger is clean, but much revenue comes by the strength of the ox" (Proverbs 14:4). In other words, it is better to have an ox (or a prophet) than not, even if it is cleaner without the ox (or prophet). The mess must be cleaned up if the Church wants the benefits of prophetic gifting.

Wesley once watched a documentary called *Yellow Fever.* It was about Brazilian miners in pursuit of gold, men who left their wives and children to go deep into the jungle and live in harsh conditions. Their job was to blast the side of a large mountain with pressurized water. As the water dislodged the dirt, it formed a river of mud that drained down the hillside. Thousands of men, standing up to their knees in muck, busily scooped up huge buckets of the mud, which they carried to the rinsers. The mud was then rinsed over and over again. Panning ever so delicately, they hoped in the end to be left with a little gold dust or, better yet, a few small golden nuggets.

After the documentary Wesley told me, "That is what we are doing! All the muck and trouble for a few small golden nuggets. Prophetic nuggets. Apples of gold in pictures of silver. Words fitly spoken from God" (see Proverbs 25:11). It takes a lot of wading and washing to get to the gold. Maybe this is why Paul wrote, "Do not treat prophecies with contempt. Test everything. Hold on to the good" (1 Thessalonians 5:20–21, NIV). To pastor the prophetic, the Church must begin by realizing that, in spite of the pitfalls, we must nurture and not despise prophecies.

The Need for Pastoring

"It was he who gave some to be apostles, some to be prophets, some to be evangelists, and some to be pastors and teachers" (Ephesians 4:11, NIV).

The prophet is not the pastor; the pastor is not the prophet. We cannot presuppose that people with prophetic gifting also possess pastoral abilities. While some may, most revelatory people are not gifted to carry the weight of leadership or pastor that which they are seeing.

Both the prophet and the pastor may be sorely tested with any outbreak of renewal and prophecy. As mentioned previously, the prophetic person will have his or her fair share of problems. But the pastors will be tested as well. Will they continue to pastor in the outpouring, or will they abdicate to others? The answer to that question will determine the effectiveness and life expectancy of a visitation.

As the early Church grew, the apostles were forced to pastor more. Paul's entire section on spiritual gifts in 1 Corinthians 12–14 is pastoral in nature. People do not handle change well. The more activity a church experiences, the more the need for pastoral care. The more movement, the more need for guidance. A floating or drifting sailboat requires little guidance, but if the winds are high and the boat is moving fast, then constant vigilance is essential. The Church needs to be pastored; the prophetic people need to be pastored, and the prophecies or prophetic messages need to be pastored.

The Need for Leadership

The leaders, too, will be tested. Will they continue to lead in the outpouring, or will they abdicate to others? Leaders cannot relinquish their role even when—might I say, especially when—the prophetic voice is strong.

The revelation of prophetic people can be so powerful and accurate that it appears the prophets have the entire mind of

Christ on the matter about which they are prophesying. Or the ecstatic manifestations can be so demonstrative that they overwhelm the leaders in charge.

When strong prophets are in the midst of a church, pastoral or apostolic leaders may become extremely intimidated. They often are afraid to lead these people who "hear from God." They think, *If God is speaking, ought we not listen?* Unfortunately, when intimidation sets in, pastors lay down their gifts—to the detriment of the Body of Christ.

"We know [see] in part, and we prophesy in part" (1 Corinthians 13:9, NIV). Letting the Spirit lead does not mean that the Spirit's leading is antithetical to His own complementary but distinct spiritual gifts of "leadership, governance and administration" (Romans 12:5–8). Structure is not the great enemy of being led by the Spirit. On the contrary, it is the bipolar extremes of too much structure or too much free form that create the problems. And the leaders are the ones who give a church structure. They are like riverbanks, which actually increase the speed of the water, or containers, which increase the water's usefulness.

Leaders, never abdicate leadership when prophecy is functioning. Lead prophets to prophesy within the biblical guidelines of time and place, guiding them when and where to prophesy, if at all. Leaders must lead.

When God is speaking through people, He is also leading through people. We all are co-laboring with Him, all using our gifts until we come to the unity of the faith.

The Need for Prophets

While it is essential that pastors pastor and leaders lead, it is equally essential that prophets prophesy. Scripture says, "Two or three prophets should speak, and the others should weigh carefully what is said" (1 Corinthians 14:29, NIV). Notice that the "prophets should speak."

Getting prophetic people to speak is an art. I have discovered that prophetic meetings need a conductor. Paul put it aptly when he likened the Church to instruments of an orchestra (see 1 Corinthians 14:7–8). An orchestra has a conductor!

In any church the people who ought to speak often do not, and the people who ought not to speak always do. I have often found that godly and gracious people are less inclined to push themselves forward. Yet they may be the very ones through whom the Lord is speaking. But there are others who say too much, and by their audacity they destroy credibility and shut down the authentic gift of prophecy in the group. So a prophetic administrator or conductor has to govern the amount of volume being produced. They have to silence the part of the band that is too noisy and increase the volume of other instruments.

Once the prophets speak, "the others should weigh carefully what is said" (1 Corinthians 14:29, NIV). Judgment of the words lies with the hearers. In our context we stress that all prophecies come under the judgment of the leaders and the listeners. Prophetic people are not necessarily responsible for the interpretation of their words and are definitely not responsible for the application of them. That responsibility lies with the leaders or with the individual(s) to whom the prophecy is given. In one respect this principle is freeing for the prophet, but it also can cause some conflict. All prophetic people must cultivate a heart of submission. This is sometimes more easily said than done.

One reason for this is that prophetic words often come with intense feelings. Like the bird in *Chicken Little*, the prophet can feel that the sky is falling or that disaster will be immediate if obedience does not follow his or her prophetic word. When I was younger, I would often fall into this trap. I would run to Wesley, who was also the pastor of our church, and say, "Wesley! Wesley! I heard from God! We have to change course, or else! All the prophets got the same word at the same time! We must do something now! Plus, we all received prophecies of the number eight, and we think it means that everything must be changed within eight days!" Wesley would calmly look at me and ask me a few penetrating questions. "So what will happen to all the kids in Sunday school if we totally change the service like you suggest? And what about . . . ?" He would generally end by saying something like, "What you are talking about is a major directional change. If it is the Lord as you say, then the elders will judge it, and it will take at least eight months to shift a thousand people to this understanding." He would bring up angles I never even thought about. At that point I would generally have a "eureka" moment along with my prophetic moment. A "spirit of *wisdom* and revelation" would descend upon me, and I would understand the bigger picture. I cannot tell you how many times I was so glad for wisdom.

Now that I am older, I rarely worry if people see "my prophetic perspective" or not. I trust God to be the Head of His Church. I try always to do my part when invited, but I do not assume leadership when it is not my sphere. I do whatever the leaders want, except compromise a prophetic word to fit a leader's desire. If I feel it is God, then I will deliver quietly to the leadership what I feel He tells me. I will not compromise on content, but I will comply with the principle of when and where I deliver the content.

Prophetic people are not responsible to see that directional words are carried out. These words may, in fact, be rejected (see Ezekiel 33:1–9). But if a prophetic person does not cultivate a submissive attitude, then they will begin to hold an offense and feel as if leadership is being disobedient to God. A serious division can be the eventual result, which is exactly the opposite of God's intended aim for the gift.

God Is Passionate for His Bride

"And God gave some to be prophets . . . until we all come to unity." After twenty years of prophesying, I am more committed

to the Body of Christ than ever. God is passionate about His Bride. I see this all the time—nation by nation, church by church, individual by individual.

Last week I was in Asia, prophesying over a group of people. One member of this group was full of anger and demonized by bitterness. When I looked at this person, God showed me not the anger, not the demons, but the hurt person under it all. And in my head I heard Him singing the children's song "Jesus Loves Me." I walked over to the person, whose eyes were trying furtively to avoid mine, put my arms around her and began to sing (even though I cannot sing), "Yes, Jesus loves you. Yes, Jesus loves you. Yes, Jesus loves you. The Bible tells me so." The anger dissolved into tears and ran down her face.

Over and over again I hear that song. He sings it regularly over me, melting my heart. He sings it over His Bride as He smoothes her wrinkles and takes out her spots.

Twenty years and thousands of prophecies later, I am slowly understanding the part that prophecy plays in bringing about unity, the knowledge of God and maturity (see Ephesians 4:13). When pastors pastor, leaders lead, teachers teach and prophets prophesy—all the gifts in their proper place—then the Bride increases in beauty, and the whole world increases in faith (see John 17:21).

Developing the Inner Life of the Prophet

11

Prophesy According to Faith

For every believer, faith is the essential starting point. We live by faith, we walk by faith, and without faith we have no hope of bringing pleasure to God: "And without faith it is *impossible to please God*, because anyone who comes to him must believe that he exists and that he rewards those who earnestly seek him" (Hebrews 11:6, NIV, emphasis mine).

So if we live to bring Him pleasure, then we need faith. And nowhere is the walk of faith more important than in the inner life of a prophet (I am talking *prophet* in the New Testament sense as in Ephesians 4:11–13).

Fear: The Opposite of Faith

The opposite of faith is fear. What people do not know, they fear and consequently reject. The fear of the unknown is what keeps many people from pursuing spiritual gifts and from pursuing their personal destinies. Christians, however, need never be afraid. We need to be wise and discerning, but not fearful. When we walk in faith, we will be able to discern the false from the true, based upon the Word of God. Prophets, in particular, need to pursue faith rather than fear.

Often I have been affected by the legendary stories of Smith Wigglesworth, who is known as "the apostle of faith." One story tells of a time when Satan himself appeared to Wigglesworth. Apparently Wigglesworth awoke in the night and actually saw the devil standing in his bedroom. Smith calmly looked over, saw it was Satan and said, "Oh, it's only you." He then rolled over in his bed and went back to sleep.[1]

This is the kind of faith that all prophets need to cultivate—faith in a God so big that the devil is comparatively insignificant. Prophets must remember that "it is only the devil" and that one prophet, Elijah, was stronger than an entire nation's worth of the false prophets of Baal. With this kind of God leading us, why should we fear anything?

Prophets must cultivate faith because they may see a lot of things in the spirit that will alarm them. Prophets must grow their faith by staring at God through His Word. "Faith comes from hearing, and hearing by the word of Christ" (Romans 10:17). The more we have the Word of God in us, the more we will respond to all things in the spirit by faith and not fear.

If prophets do not cultivate an inner life of faith, then how they articulate what they discern in the spirit could promote fear rather than faith in the Church. I cannot underscore how important this is for prophets. I have seen whole churches taken out by a small group of fearful prophets.

Turning the Negative into Faith

When I train budding prophets, I like to ask them, "How many of you have ever seen or felt a demon, or felt the strong presence of evil?" Almost invariably 100 percent of the hands in the class go up. Then I ask them, "How many of you have had a vision of Jesus or have seen angels?" Generally only about one-third of the class raises their hands. As in natural life, so it is with the spiritual life. For prophets in particular, it appears to be easier to see the negative than it is to see the positive.

In the initial days of our church's prophetic outpouring, we so loved the presence of God that we would meet night after night to pray and prophesy—just as the early Church did. The "watchmen" among us would prophesy regularly about the various dangers that the enemy plotted against us. Generally they were accurate words, and listening to them saved us from a lot of potential harm.

After a short while, however, I noticed that these "watchmen" prophets would discern quite regularly dangers, negative things and the sins of others. This pastor had that problem, that elder did this, this sister had a spirit of thus and such. Sadly, most of the discernment was true. But as time progressed I became troubled by it. I observed that this discernment was causing an elitist spirit. Certain people were deemed acceptable, but others were "Xed." The "Xed" ones were unwelcome in the prayer meetings—even though some of them were pastors! I tried to voice my disagreement with the way things were going, but I was the odd one out. Everyone else could see all these negative things, so where was my discernment? Even I became suspect by the rest of the group, and my leadership was undermined.

Smith Wigglesworth addressed this issue in one of his books. He chose the way of faith, so that even when he operated in the gift of discerning of spirits he never saw people through the eyes of fear or suspicion. He noted that God gave the gift of discernment, but he also noted the purpose of spiritual discernment.

"To another discerning of spirits." There is a vast difference between natural discernment and spiritual. When it comes to natural discernment you will find many people loaded with it, and they can see so many faults in others. To such the words of Christ in the sixth chapter of Luke surely apply,

"Why beholdest thou the mote that is in thy brother's eye, but perceivest not the beam that is in thine own eye?" If you want to manifest natural discernment, focus the same on yourself for at least twelve months, and you will see so many faults in yourself that you will never want to fuss about the faults of another.[2]

I wondered how this powerful move of the Holy Spirit in our church could be so negative. I began to pray. "Lord, why are we seeing all these sins? I know You love everyone, so when You give me discernment please also show me what You love about this person/ministry." After several months of praying that prayer, I began to prophesy from an entirely different perspective. I had faith to see people's potential destiny, not just their actual failures. It dawned on me that because of His blood covering, Jesus looks at me with eyes of faith. He does not see all my sins; rather, He stares into my future, knowing that "from the foundation of the world" there were "good works" foreordained for me to do (see Ephesians 2:8–10). From this revelation, my perspective about others changed radically. I entered into *His* faith for His followers, and I began to see potential and destiny in almost everyone for whom I prayed.

Prophesying God's Faith for Others

In the natural world, Gideon was not a warrior. As a matter of fact, no one was more aware of this than Gideon himself. Gideon's self-perception was pitiful: "[Gideon] said to Him, 'O Lord, how shall I deliver Israel? Behold, my family is the least in Manasseh, and I am the youngest in my father's house'" (Judges 6:15).

Gideon thought that because Manasseh was the smallest tribe in Israel and because his family was the lowest family in the smallest tribe, and because he was the youngest one in the lowest family, the Lord must have picked the wrong guy. But apparently God was not concerned with Gideon's inabilities and insignificance. The angel of the Lord prophesied to weak, oppressed, intimidated Gideon and said, "You are a valiant warrior!" This angel, sent by God, completely ignored Gideon's present reality and prophesied his powerful future.

Amazingly, after I began to pray daily, "Show me what You love about people," my prophetic sight was also greatly enlarged. I, too, began to see the incredible destinies that God created for even the most broken people. The understanding I gleaned from praying that prayer taught me one of the most valuable lessons about how to use the gift of prophecy. I learned that not only does God love me all the time, but He also believes I can do all things through His strength. He thinks I am a world-changer. He thinks that nothing is impossible for me when I believe in Him! And He also believes the same about every one of His children because He indwells us and He knows what He can do. His strength is actually perfected in weakness (see 2 Corinthians 12:9), so natural weakness becomes an asset and not a hindrance. All God needs is people who will agree with *Him*, and not with the labels our families or society place on us.

Learning to Let the False Mature

When prophets do not prophesy from a perspective of faith, what they see may alarm them. Their responses to prophetic revelation will either be fear ("Something bad is going to happen") or suspicion ("God cannot use that person/church because of all the bad stuff they are doing").

Prophets should look to our Savior as our example in how to handle these responses. Jesus was not suspicious or fearful about anything He saw. And He did not try to fix things all at once. In the parable of the wheat and the tares (see Matthew 3:12), He demonstrated that sometimes you have to let the false grow until it matures to the point where everyone can see it before it can be fixed.

I try to teach prophets this lesson because sometimes they discern danger or weaknesses in others and feel a great urgency to point them out. But when God allows a prophet to see somebody's sins, it usually is not because God wants to deal with the "sinner." Rather, God allows the prophet to discern weakness in order to give the prophet a "faith test." Most often God is testing the prophet and not, as the prophet surmises, testing the "sinner" with such knowledge. He wants to see how the prophet's heart will handle knowledge about the failures of others. Will the prophet prophesy in faith in spite of what he or she sees? Sometimes the prophet's job is simply to intercede for the opposite of the negative thing.

Prophesying out of Unbelief

The opposite of prophesying according to faith is prophesying out of unbelief. Unbelief has power, too. If prophets prophesy sin and failure, even though they may be true, they give a curse instead of a blessing. When prophets use "natural discernment" (to quote Smith Wigglesworth above), they decree what is instead of what shall be or what could be.

Joshua and Caleb were the only two of twelve spies who came back to Moses and the nation of Israel with a good report of the Promised Land (see Numbers 13–14). Even though all twelve spies knew this was the land God promised them, ten spies came back with a bad report. Only two could see the huge grapes, the milk and honey, the massive potential of the Promised Land (see Numbers 13:27–29; 14:7–9). Although the grapes were huge, to the ten spies the giants were evidently much bigger. But Joshua and Caleb saw the grapes. It takes a lot of faith to see grapes when there are giants. Prophets are to look for grapes, not giants. We are to look for the good so that our prophecies edify, comfort and exhort.

One time I was talking with a senior prophet from America who consistently gives incredibly accurate words. We were talking about the state of the American Church when he suddenly blurted out, "We have got to get the prophets out of the second heaven." When I asked him what he meant by that statement, he replied, "'Satan walks about like a roaring lion, seeking whom he may devour' [see 1 Peter 5:8]. Satan has a plan, and it is destruction. The Bible is clear that we are not to be 'unaware of his schemes' [2 Corinthians 2:11, NIV]. But we must make sure that the prophets are not prophesying the devil's plans. Prophets have to rise above seeing only the devil's intentions and begin to prophesy the will of God!" I thought that was a godly perspective. We must not prophesy curses over others, but blessings.

A pearl always lies in the middle of the dirt. Jesus demonstrated that it is worth buying the whole field for that one treasure. The prophet looks for the pearl, calls it out, names it and prophesies to it, and sometimes the dirt drops off on its own. At other times issues may have to be addressed, but when prophets see the pearls, they see the dirt differently. Rather than being an obstacle, the dirt is merely something to be overcome.

No believer is doomed to stay in his or her sins. Every single one of us can overcome! We overcome "by the blood of the Lamb"—by what Jesus has done. It is possible for every single believer to overcome because Jesus has overcome everything for us. And this is the victory that overcomes the world—our faith (see 1 John 5:4).

Seeing Others through God's Eyes

No one has more faith than God. He is full of faith for each one of us. He sees us so differently than we see ourselves. If we prophesy according to our level of faith (see Romans 12:6), what does that look like? What do you see when you look at

171

people? At the Church? Do you always see the bad, or do you see the good and the potential? It is true that throughout the Bible, God gives warnings through His prophets, but even warnings can be delivered in faith.

In some places I have visited, no matter which way I turned all I could see was evil—really wicked places that have literally given themselves over to pornography, violence, drugs and poverty. One such place was a city in Siberia. Pornography was everywhere. The billboards displayed naked women, and the coffee shops offered porn magazines on the tables. The immorality had so penetrated the culture that its effects were evident even in the church we visited. The pastor's wife had one of the lowest cut dresses I had ever seen on a Christian leader. The dress code both for men and women was more like that of a nightclub than a church. I did not even want to speak there because I was afraid of what I might blurt out. I was agitated inside and not confident I could speak properly into the situation. My mother had taught me, "If you cannot say anything nice, then don't say anything at all," so I thought I had better just be silent. How could I speak with faith to a city that so evidently "tolerated that woman Jezebel" (see Revelation 2:20)? So I went to my hotel room and began to pray, *God, what do You want me to say?*

I opened my Bible to Revelation 2 and began to pray through what God spoke to the church of Thyatira—the church that "tolerated that woman Jezebel."

> And to the angel of the church in Thyatira write: The Son of God, who has eyes like a flame of fire, and His feet are like burnished bronze, says this: "I know your deeds, and your love and faith and service and perseverance, and that your deeds of late are greater than at first. But I have this against you, that you tolerate the woman Jezebel, who calls herself a prophetess, and she teaches and leads My bond-servants astray so that they commit acts of immorality and eat things sacrificed to idols. I gave her time to repent, and she does not want to repent of her immorality. Behold, I will throw her on

a bed of sickness, and those who commit adultery with her into great tribulation, unless they repent of her deeds. And I will kill her children with pestilence, and all the churches will know that I am He who searches the minds and hearts; and I will give to each one of you according to your deeds. But I say to you, the rest who are in Thyatira, who do not hold this teaching, who have not known the deep things of Satan, as they call them—I place no other burden on you. Nevertheless what you have, hold fast until I come. He who overcomes, and he who keeps My deeds until the end, to him I will give authority over the nations; and he shall rule them with a rod of iron, as the vessels of the potter are broken to pieces, as I also have received authority from My Father; and I will give him the morning star. He who has an ear, let him hear what the Spirit says to the churches."

Revelation 2:18–29

As I read these verses, understanding and faith poured into my heart. How did God see Thyatira, the very church that "tolerated Jezebel"? First God saw all the good things Thyatira did: her deeds, her love, her faith, her perseverance, her greater deeds (see verse 19). And He recognized them: "Thyatira, I know you! I know your deeds—all of them. And I even see that you are doing more good deeds now than you ever did!" And then God saw Thyatira's destiny: authority over the nations, supreme rulership and the morning star (see verses 26–28). God knew what Thyatira could do. Within her was the power to affect nations. And God also saw Thyatira's weaknesses: her compromise, her immorality and her idolatry. He spoke to it as well. All Thyatira had to do was overcome this one little Jezebel spirit in order to move into her destiny.

When I saw all of this in the Word, I got it! I suddenly had faith and knew how to prophesy to this situation. I asked God to reveal to me this Siberian church's present good works and its destiny, which He immediately did. By the time I got to church that night to speak, I could hardly wait to prophesy. I had lots of good stuff for which I could commend this apostolic center in Siberia. I also saw lots of potential for this church to do much good in their region. With this as a backdrop I was also able to address the issue of immorality.

At the end of my prophecy that night, I declared that God wanted the church to be in daily prayer for her leaders because He had planned such powerful destinies for them. I called forward the pastors and leaders and asked the whole church to join as one and fight for the leadership in prayer. I had all one thousand people commit to pray daily for an overcoming spirit and a spirit of wisdom and revelation in the leadership. Suddenly the power of God broke into the congregation. In the balcony, people began falling to the ground under the power of the Holy Spirit—weeping, crying, calling out to the Lord and receiving visions. The leaders for whom we were praying up front, who had been reserved and cold up to this point, began trembling and weeping as the congregation called out to God on their behalf. It was an amazing spiritual breakthrough.

Years later I heard that the leadership in that region had planted many other works and led many Kingdom initiatives there. God was able to move powerfully through this church. Would this have happened if I had cursed the place? If I had pointed out only the bad? Because God gave me His faith for this church and because I listened to Him, I was able to speak truth and blessing to this church, and they were able to receive it. And subsequently, the ground was fertile and ready for Him to use this group of believers in incredibly powerful ways.

Cultivating Faith

We have different gifts, according to the grace given us. If a man's gift is prophesying, let him use it in proportion to his faith.

Romans 12:6, NIV

174

In order to see the world through God's eyes, prophets must cultivate hearts of faith. A few years ago our family was staying at a friend's house. Over the weekend while we all were away, the house was robbed. We came home Sunday night to a house that had been completely torn apart. The lock on the door was broken, all the drawers were emptied with their contents strewn about the rooms and the closets were turned upside down. We called the police and spent the rest of the day cleaning up the mess the robbers had made.

That night I had a dream. In my dream the thieves came back. The dream was quite vivid, and I felt that the spirit motivating the robbers was in the house with me, sneaking through the door, creeping down the hallway and slipping into the room where Wesley and I slept. In the dream the robber came over to the bed, raised his hand, which held a knife, and started to bring it down toward me. At that moment I jumped up, startling the robber so that he ran down the hall. But I did not stop there. I was filled with a powerful spirit of faith, and I knew that I had more power than the thief did. So I kept chasing him out of the house, down the street and all the way out of town. The thief was far more afraid of me than I was of him. By the time I woke up, the thief was long gone.

That was only a dream. But God also has given me a similar spirit of faith to undertake direct encounters with demonic spirits. A couple of summers ago I was in Tanzania, Africa, teaching at a pastors' school. At the end of the school the leaders took us on a one-day safari. We had a great day, and that night we stayed in a place near the base of the great Kilimanjaro mountain. In the middle of the night I had a demonic encounter. The only way I can describe it is that I felt my spirit was being pulled from my body. I got up and began to pray, calling on the name of Jesus. Within a short while the encounter was over, but it took me a while to get back to sleep.

Over breakfast the next morning I told some of the Tanzanian pastors what had happened. One of the pastors was from the Masai tribe. He listened with interest to my story, and when I finished he told me one of the wildest stories I have ever heard. He said, "I know the reason you had that demonic encounter. It is because of the work you do to save orphans.[3] Mount Kilimanjaro has a long history of child sacrifice, and you upset the demons that kill children. They were mad at you because you save children, and they kill them." I knew nothing of the history of the region and was intrigued by his response. I listened quietly as he continued.

"One morning I was in prayer for my church," he said, "and the Lord impressed upon me an urgent need to visit a particular member of my congregation. So I rose from prayer and went directly to his home. When I arrived, the husband had a knife in his hand and was trying to kill his wife. I looked into his crazed eyes and saw that he was clearly under the influence of demonic spirits. So I bound them and cast them out. When he was back in his right mind I asked him what happened. He told me that the night before some spirits came to him and pulled his spirit out of his body. They took his spirit man to a high mountain and forced him to drink blood. When they brought him back to his body, he was completely demonized. And that is when he tried to kill his wife."

Now I do not really know what to make of all these things. I do know I had a demonic encounter. Nothing else like that has ever happened to me before or since. And this pastor just matter-of-factly told me his story, which I can neither corroborate nor disclaim. All I know is that God is real, heaven is real, the devil is real and hell is real. And I know that we must have faith in God's greater power in every circumstance.

I tell these stories to illustrate that faith can be cultivated. "Greater" is one of my favorite prayers: "Greater is He who is in you than he who is in the world" (1 John 4:4). God is so much greater, and His greatness works in every believer. As prophets, we must cultivate a heart of faith so that we can face with confidence any spiritual situation in which the Lord places us. Like Smith Wigglesworth, even when we face the devil himself we must do so with a heart of faith that knows, beyond a shadow of a doubt, that He in us is greater.

Releasing Destinies

When we prophesy in faith, we can change even the futures of others by naming their divine destinies. Ecstatic prophecy, in particular, seems to release gifts in others. Literally hundreds of people have told me, "After you prophesied over me, I started healing the sick," or ". . . I started prophesying," or ". . . I started . . ." Often when I ask if they did those things before the prophecy, they say, "No, nothing like that ever happened to me before."

Last year I was in Harrisburg, Pennsylvania, speaking on healing. I explained that I am just beginning to see medically documented healings. Afterward a man walked up to me and said, "I thought you always moved in healing because you were the one who released the gift of healing in me. Several years ago you picked me out of a crowd and said that God would use me to heal the sick. Right after that I started seeing healing miracles. I have participated in healing crusades in many countries." When I asked him if he had healed the sick prior to that, he said, "No."

If I were to examine this phenomenon and try to deduce why ecstatic prophecy looses gifts in others, I would have to describe it this way: It appears that the heightened "rushing" of the Spirit that occurs in ecstatic states sets in motion spiritual gifts in others. It seems to loose or create the manifestation of the Spirit (i.e., gifts—see 1 Corinthians 12). Prophecy, healing, preaching with boldness and many other gifts are set in motion from ecstatic prophecy.

I hear testimonies of released destinies so regularly that I desire more faith to see what God sees in His people. God is great! He can do anything with anybody! I am regularly in awe of what God has done in and through me—and the rest of His Church. There is no one like Him (see Psalm 86:8), and He is worthy of worship for the millions of things He does daily through the weakest of vessels.

Changing Lives

Prophecy can change even the most broken of lives. A couple of months ago I was in Europe speaking at a conference. At the end of my session a woman walked up to me, looked me straight in the eye, put one finger in the air in front of my face and said, "I am one! I am one!" I had no idea what she meant. She continued, "You were here in my country about three years ago. You preached and then prayed impartation of the Spirit of prophecy on all the people who came to the conference. I was in that meeting, and at the time I had MPD (Multiple Personality Disorder). I was fractured into over one hundred personalities. After your prayer I went upstairs to a small room in the conference center, and as I walked into the room Jesus appeared before me. He held His arms open wide and beckoned me to come to Him. I walked over to where He was, and as I came close He took me in His arms. When He unfolded His arms and set me back on the floor, I was completely sane and in my right mind. Now I am one! I am one!" This woman's current pastor and his wife had accompanied her when she came to tell me the story, and they verified everything she said, adding that their church had since seen many healings of emotional and psychological disorders. This story merely illustrates to me again how God can take the most broken, worst-case scenarios and bring healing and life to every situation.

Changing Religious Mindsets

Prophecy changes lives in another way. It is a powerful tool to break through false theologies and religious mindsets.

Wesley and I were converted from dispensational theology to faith in charismatic theology through one encounter with a prophet. It happened at a Christian meeting on my university campus. Prior to this meeting Wesley had been preaching against prophecy in many Plymouth Brethren churches. But we had come into contact with some charismatic Christians who were so zealous that for the first time in my life I thought, *Well, these charismatics are actually saved. Not only are they saved, but they are also more zealous than I, so they must have something.* We were watching them and definitely were affected by them, but we did not want to be led into false teaching. So we began to pray seriously about what to do.

One day Wesley was in the shower praying silently, *What is going on? Is this charismatic stuff from You, God, or not?* That night we decided to go again to the Christian meeting on campus but entered late. When we walked into the meeting, a prophet was already preaching. We had never seen him before, but we discovered later that he had come from the States and did not know who we were. We sat in the back. By the end of his sermon he started saying, "God has a plan for you, and you and you . . ." He began speaking directly to people's lives. And then he said, "And you!" He pointed at us in the back and asked us to stand up. He spoke to Wesley and said, "You, young man, have been asking Me a question." And then he quoted a Scripture: " 'The gift of prophecy is for edification, exhortation and comfort.' You have been asking Me, 'Are these things for today?' " This prophet could never have known the contents of that silent prayer Wesley had asked the Lord that very afternoon in the shower. Wesley was dumbstruck. The prophet continued, "Not only are they for today, but I have also laid them out for you on a silver platter," and he started to prophesy into our destiny. And we were totally changed from a prophetic word.

This is the Spirit of prophecy—the testimony of Jesus. Who is He in you? When prophets understand the answer to this question, they will see the power of prophesying "according to faith," not according to what they discern in the natural.

Faith Activates Prophecy

Over and over in the Bible God trains His prophets to see beyond the natural. Many times in Scripture we see Him asking his prophets, "What do you see?" (see Jeremiah 1:11, 13; 24:3; Amos 7:8; 8:2; Zechariah 4:2; 5:2). A prophet may see dry bones, but if he or she keeps looking, then those dry bones can turn into an exceeding great army (see Ezekiel 37). This is prophesying according to faith.

Faith does not come from the outside; it is cultivated from the interior heart of a prophet. If prophets are going to serve the Body of Christ with the gift of prophecy, we cannot wait for the faith of the people. We need to develop our own faith. Remember: "Prophesy according to your faith" (Romans 12:6). Faith is the commodity that activates prophecy.

See as God sees. Believe for the greater works that are beyond the natural circumstances. You will be amazed how faith ignites the hearers and how impossible things are made possible.

12

PROPHESY IN LOVE

For the testimony of Jesus is the spirit of prophecy" (Revelation 19:10). Jesus' nature, therefore, or testimony, is revealed when true prophecy is in operation. Prophecy is about Him! I do not mean that the content of every prophecy is about Jesus. What I mean is that the effect of true prophecy should be that something of the nature of Jesus is revealed. Perhaps a prophet gives someone a specific word of knowledge that divulges how intimately Jesus knows that person. Or perhaps the Spirit of prophecy causes the presence of God to manifest so tangibly that the recipients fall down and exclaim, "Surely God is among you!" The end result of true prophecy is a deeper disclosure of Jesus.

If the primary purpose of prophecy is to make Him known, how can we do it if we ourselves do not know Him well? Since prophecy is His testimony, then knowing Him must be the central focus of a prophet's life. I believe, therefore, that the single most important discipline for developing a prophetic heart is the practice of "beholding Jesus."

Prophets Who Beheld Jesus

Elijah was a man "just like us. [But] he prayed" (James 5:17, NIV). Prayer caused Elijah to have faith to change nations, to face down false prophets, to believe for rain in the middle of a drought, to raise the dead, to prophesy to hostile kings. Through prayer, Elijah came to know God. When nobody else was praying, he got down on his knees and prayed until a tiny cloud turned into a torrential downpour. Prayer was a lifestyle for the prophet Elijah, not a fleeting fancy. As a result, knowledge of God came through every prophetic act he did. The prophecies and prophetic demonstrations in Elijah's life teach us more about God Himself.

Prayer was also a lifestyle for the prophet Daniel. Nothing could alter his practice of thrice-daily prayer. Even when threatened with death, "he got down on his knees and prayed, giving thanks to his God, just as he had done before" (Daniel 6:10, NIV).

These great prophets had capacity to deliver eternal knowledge about God through prophetic utterance because they spent time in His presence. The more they beheld Him, the more He revealed Himself to them.

Deeper Love, Deeper Understanding

God gives sovereign gifts of prophecy. But there also is a correlation between one's personal pursuit of the knowledge of God and the capacity to both contain it and reveal it.

When a prophetic word is given, it contains certain spiritual "tones." This principle has a biblical precedent. When Jesus taught, for example, He clearly spoke with a different tone than the scribes. "When Jesus had finished these words, the crowds were amazed at His teaching; for He was teaching them as one having authority, and not as their scribes" (Matthew 7:28–29). Jesus had authority, and when He spoke everyone noticed the difference between what He said and what the other teachers said.

Similarly, in the past twenty years I have heard many people prophesy, and I have noticed that when a person has a deep relationship with Jesus his or her words carry more weight. When he or she prophesies, the power of the prophetic word shatters the atmosphere. The entire congregation hears it and is moved by it. One prophecy can shift the whole service. I might not even get to preach because the prophecy has shattered the spiritual atmosphere, brought us into the presence of God and prepared the way for Him to take over sovereignly.

The person who does not have a deep relationship with Jesus, on the other hand, has no authority in his or her words. Even though the gift of prophecy may operate in this person, the words go unheard. The words die as they leave the mouth.

I have tested this phenomenon repeatedly. When I go to teach in a church, I listen intently to any prophecy given to hear what the Spirit is saying. I usually try to discern what the Father is saying to a church or region, so I am keen to hear prophetic words in services. Many times the prophecy is identical to the topic on which the Lord has told me to speak. So I am encouraged.

Some words, however, are really hard to hear. Their delivery carries no weight. Even when the content is good, no one hears it. When I get up to speak, I ask, "Who remembers what the prophecy said?" As little as five minutes later, no one in the entire church building can remember the content of the prophetic word.

God gives gifts to everyone as He deems fit (see 1 Corinthians 12:11), but authority is earned through relationship. He will disclose Himself to the one who knows Him and loves

Him, but He will not disclose Himself to everyone (see John 2:24; 14:21–22). Deeper revelation comes from deeper love. Deeper understanding comes from beholding.

Love Comes from Knowing

It is possible, therefore, to operate in a prophetic anointing, understanding all mysteries and all knowledge, yet not have love (see 1 Corinthians 13:2). If a person does not pursue an intimate relationship with Jesus, then he or she does not know Him, and His love is not flowing through that person. The result of no love in the heart is that the person is nothing before God, and this is tragic.

Over and over again I have seen prophetic people who know so much knowledge—even sometimes mysteries—about both God and people, but they are destroyed because they have pursued the gift and not the love. I have watched prophets prophesy details about a person's life or know mysteries about them, but rather than producing increased love, this knowledge has been the excuse to cut off a member of the Body of Christ from relationship.

There is a vast difference, then, between the anointing and the motivation of the heart. People look at the anointing, but God looks at the heart.

Three Characteristics That Separate Prophecy from Love

How does prophecy operate separately from love? I have witnessed several answers to this question.

First, prophets can be easily wounded. If these wounds are not healed, they color the way prophets see the world. Wounded prophets can receive accurate knowledge but wrongly impugn motive or wrongly interpret this knowledge because they are seeing the knowledge through their wounding. Wounds affect perspective, which in turn affects love. Prophets, therefore, need to be healed; otherwise they will not see purely.

"To the pure, all things are pure; but to those who are defiled and unbelieving, nothing is pure, but both their mind and their conscience are defiled" (Titus 1:15). When prophets are defiled from wounds and rejection, they become fearful and critical. The result is that they prophesy accurate knowledge out of hearts of fear. And when prophets prophesy out of fear they open themselves up to the Jezebel spirit. This infamous spirit seeks to bring all the prophets under her influence, to lead them into immorality and ultimately to destroy them (see 1 Kings 18:4, 19; Revelation 2:20).

Many times we ourselves do not know we are as wounded as we are. Recently I was talking to a woman who told me, "I had no idea I was as angry as I was, but I knew that when I began to prophesy, I would generally prophesy judgment. It was not until I got some inner healing that I realized the pain in my heart clouded the way I looked at things. I could not see purely, and I could not see clearly." Jesus spoke to this when He said, "The eye is the lamp of the body; so then if your eye is clear, your whole body will be full of light. But if your eye is bad, your whole body will be full of darkness. If then the light that is in you is darkness, how great is the darkness!" (Matthew 6:22–23).

Second, prophecy can operate separately from love because of unforgiveness. When prophets get hurt—and we will get hurt—we must learn to forgive. I often pray, "Lord, when things happen to me that hurt me, please help me forget the sin of others the way You forget my sin. Help me to 'remember them no more'" (see Jeremiah 31:34). I do not pray necessarily to forget the experience, because I can learn from the experience, but I do pray to forget the sting of it so that I have nothing in my heart against people or situations.

Third, prophecy can operate separately from love because the prophet has a heart of judgment. I shared in the last chapter how God allows prophets to see the problems of others not so we can judge them but so we can help them out of their problems. The prophet who does not walk in intimacy with the Lord runs the risk of stopping at the judgment.

In the early days of the prophetic outpouring in our church, we received lots of accurate revelation—but our knowledge did not lead to love. A group of us in the prophetic department used to collect our discernment about other people and then talk about it in groups. "Did you see such and such about so and so?" "Yes, I saw exactly the same thing!" "I even got a dream about that. Oh, something really bad is going on there." Our hearts would fill with pride that we all heard the same prophecy and that we were so accurate. Not only were we not loving, but we were also downright unkind. Then we would justify the fact that we separated ourselves from them. We took special delight in targeting other pastors and leaders with our prophetic judgment.

It did not take long for a major division in the spirit to occur between the prophetic people and many of the pastors. In addition, we also successfully shrunk the prophetic group because we deemed many not good enough to pray with us. We went from a bunch to only a few. We spiritualized our pride and our elitism.

One of the best things that ever happened to me in the area of prophecy was also one of the worst things that ever happened to me. I became the recipient of prophetic discernment. A group of prophetic people saw my sins, called me into a room, sat me down and said, "Stacey, we have discerned certain things, and we are concerned about your prophetic gift."

I responded, "Okay, what have you discerned?" They were not exactly sure what the specific problem was, but they were sure "something was wrong with my prophetic gift." Of course, I did not want to have anything wrong with the way I prophesied, so I asked again, "Please tell me what it is." But nobody knew for sure.

Suddenly the Lord gave someone a word of knowledge: "This thing will not be broken off Stacey until she cries." At that point, because they thought God was giving them permission to "break me," they sat me down and told me everything wrong with me all at once. Soon the prophecy came to pass. I was not just crying—I was sobbing. Because the prophets took my tears as confirmation that the Lord was dealing with me (the more I cried, the better), they kept going. It was pretty brutal.

From this painful experience I learned possibly the best lesson I have ever learned in how to prophesy. I learned to ask for the heart of God along with prophetic knowledge and mysteries. I wanted to hear God's heart as well as God's words. My only prayer for a long season was, "Lord, I know You love people all the time, even when they sin. The Bible says that 'even when they were yet sinners, You died for them' (see Romans 5:8). You love sinners. So I want You to show me what You love about people."

After months of praying that prayer, everything changed. A transformation took place in my heart for people. I could look at anybody, even the most broken of people, and see first all the great things God wanted to do in and through them. I could see their destinies, "the good works that were prepared in advance for them" (see Ephesians 2:10). God caused me to long for others to overcome. I began to feel that if they won, then I won, and if they lost, I lost.

In the context of their destinies, God would sometimes show me the danger zones in their lives that could keep them from attaining all God had prepared for them. But the weakness had a context of greatness, and I knew God had a way of escape for every temptation. Even the fact that God showed the weakness to me was proof of His patient love and kindness. He only showed me the knowledge because He wanted to help them overcome it.

These three things, then—wounding, unforgiveness and judgment—can affect the prophet's ability to prophesy. It is so important for prophets to deal with the logs in their own eyes before they call out the specks in other people's eyes. If we are hurt or bitter, our delivery of prophecy will be skewed and people will end up feeling that God is angry with them or is against them. This is not God's purpose in prophecy. God's purpose is love.

Prophesying through Eyes of Love

True prophetic revelation always leads to love, not away from love. "Love is patient, love is kind . . . it does not seek its own" (1 Corinthians 13:4–5). These beautiful words teach us how to prophesy well. When I train prophets, I make them meditate on each attribute of love. Then I ask them, "If love is patient, then how do you prophesy patiently? If love is kind, then how do you prophesy kindly?" And so on.

The only true way to learn to love is to behold Love Himself. God is love. Nothing can separate us from His love. The perfection of His love casts out our fears. He is omnipotent, high above every principality and power, so we do not need to be afraid. His name is above all other names. He is omniscient. He knows everything about us. He knows everything we have ever done, thought or felt—and everything we ever will do, think or feel. And in spite of this knowledge, He loves us. How can we not grow in love when we behold Him? He is for us, so who can be against us? He is love.

The entire earthly life of Jesus demonstrated this love. Behold Jesus when He interacted with sinners. He was not afraid of them. He ate and drank with them. He stopped others from stoning them. "Whatsoever things are pure . . . think on these things" (Philippians 4:8, KJV).

When we behold the love of God, we grow in love for mankind. When we are rooted and grounded in the love of God, fear dissipates and we become free to see things the way God does—with eyes of faith and a heart of love for every person. This is why we must spend so much time beholding the love of God. We have to train our spirits to behold God. Then we will become like Him. And we will deliver God's words with God's heart.

13

PROPHESY IN UNITY

Ecstatic prophecy (possession trance) can happen to individuals, but as we saw in biblical and revival history, the Holy Spirit also possesses groups of people at the same time. New Testament prophets almost always worked in teams, either with other prophets (see 1 Corinthians 14:29), with teachers (see Acts 13:1), with apostles (see Luke 11:49; Acts 11:26; Ephesians 2:20; 2 Peter 3:2) or with all the five gifts together, building for a common goal (see Ephesians 4:11–13).

Over my twenty years of prophetic ministry, I have observed an interesting phenomenon. While it is not always the case, more often than not a prophet's initial prophetic encounter sets in motion a ministry style. The initial experience often determines the presentation, whether that prophet gravitates toward a solitary life and a "Lone Ranger" ministry style, or whether he or she is more community-oriented and prefers to prophesy in groups. Both styles are valid and have biblical precedent. But since the coming prophetic outpouring is going to happen to "all flesh" (see Acts 2:17–20), we need to concentrate on working together in unity and prophesying in teams.

Our Initial Group Ecstatic Experience

Although my initial ecstatic experience was as an individual, I subsequently experienced a prophetic outpouring with the leadership team of our Baptist church. This outpouring changed our collective lives and the corporate life of our church.

It happened at a Christmas house party in 1987. We all were together, celebrating the goodness and blessing of God. Around 10:00 P.M. an elder suggested that we spend a short time in prayer. As it was a Christmas party, we all felt more like playing than praying, so the suggestion went unheeded. But the elder persisted: "We should thank God for the year." So finally we settled down. The presence of God came powerfully into the room. Without warning one of our Baptist pastors began to shake. Suddenly an elder, as if hit on the top of his head by a huge fist, was struck down into the couch. Then he rocketed back up and out into the center of the room, shaking and speaking in tongues. Next, to my astonishment, I was also catapulted off the couch into the center of the room where I began to shake violently and speak in tongues. We were seized, as if by some unseen hand, and shaken like puppets on the end of a string. As we were bouncing in the center of the room, another burst of power hit us simultaneously. According to observers, "At the exact same moment all three of them jolted, their legs flew out from under them, and they were thrown onto the floor on their backs—all the while speaking in tongues. Fear and awe gripped our souls. Some of us cried out. Space does not permit a complete description of how we wept, repented, rebuked any possible false spirits, pled the blood of Jesus and cried out for protection. Although we knew that this was God, we had never experienced anything even remotely like this before! We were conservative evangelicals!"

Next, the three of us who had been shaking began to prophesy and speak the secrets of people's hearts. Some were words of exhortation, and some were words of praise. The sense of dread and awe that filled the room was indescribable. Sometimes we were in shock, sometimes we were laughing and sometimes we fell on our faces with our noses pressed into the carpet. Steve Clarke, an elder from a Brethren background, said, "Surely I would have run out the door, but they were between the door and me, and I was afraid to go by them."

The encounter lasted over four hours. We all staggered out of that episode at about 2:30 A.M. Wesley says he remembers so clearly going outside to start up the cold car, the words of a Christmas carol playing through his mind: "The stars were brightly shining. It was the night of our dear Savior's birth." He looked up and thought, *I'll never eat another Big Mac as long as I live.* What he meant by this strange response was: "Surely I have been to the mountaintop like Moses. How can I ever function on the mundane level again?" The same was true for the rest of us. We all knew we would never be the same again, and we drove home in awe.

A month later a similar event took place involving the same people, only this time the phenomena were greater in number and varied. Prophetic motions were enacted in the bodies of some. Common manifestations were blowing, chopping and waving over the individuals receiving prayer. Sometimes the one prophesying would be bent over backward. When a word of exhortation or rebuke was given, the speaker would laugh or clap his hands, or his legs might make sharp kicking motions. Strange as it may seem, as the group brought in and prayed for more and more people, these new people would evidence the same manifestations and effects—even though they had never seen or experienced these manifestations before. Eventually about forty to fifty individuals were anointed in this way. Each was seized by the power of God and physically shaken, and this physical manifestation often was accompanied by prophecy. When interviewed later, these people said they "were overwhelmed and engulfed by the sweetness of God." Every spiritual sense they had was heightened to a higher level. During and after these impartations, almost everyone testified to having God communicate directly from His Spirit to their spirits by way of visions, pictures and words.

Some of our group began to move strongly in the gift of discerning spirits. They became competent in naming the spirits and speaking to them. Some could even see spirits with their physical eyes and could describe their appearances. During meetings others from our church would see angels that directed them in the ministry of words of knowledge and healing. Still others had open visions accompanied by great spiritual power and anointing. Almost all of these came in the context of worship and prayer. The result was ongoing renewal (and even a mini-revival) with the demonized being released, the lost saved and the non-committed convicted to a deeper walk. The accounts of these experiences alone could fill a book.

Our leadership team soon opened up ecstatic prophecy to the entire church. It began to spread like a summer brush fire. We began to hold prayer meetings virtually every night of the week, with special ministry nights on weekends. The Lord so absolutely captivated us that all we wanted to do was pray. For the next six months we spent on average 25 to 40 hours a week in prayer meetings. Every time we would worship and pray, powerful displays of God's presence would take place. Repentance spread to everyone who came, regardless of denomination or lack thereof. A number of Bible college students in our city were so convicted that they began to go to their dean and college president and confess serious sins. Though some had to be expelled from school for a time, they counted it worthwhile, as they were coming clean with God. More began to get saved. We had a series of baptism services with as many as 50 to 75 people being baptized in a day.

Our personal testimony underscores the phenomenon of ecstatic prophecy falling on groups of people at the same time. When ecstasy happens to groups, however, the group dynamics change considerably.

Moses and Joshua

In the Bible, the first example of the transferability of ecstatic prophecy is seen in the life of Moses. God literally took part of the Spirit that was upon Moses and put it on the seventy elders. Moses' individual experience became a corporate one.

> Then the LORD came down in the cloud and spoke to him; and He took of the Spirit who was upon him and placed Him upon the seventy elders. And when the Spirit rested upon them, they prophesied. But they did not do it again. But two men had remained in the camp; the name of one was Eldad and the name of the other Medad. And the Spirit rested upon them (now they were among those who had been registered, but had not gone out to the tent), and they prophesied in the camp. So a young man ran and told Moses and said, "Eldad and Medad are prophesying in the camp."
>
> Numbers 11:25–27

Immediately after this transfer of Spirit, one of the older prophets became somewhat territorial. Look at Joshua's attitude:

> Then Joshua the son of Nun, the attendant of Moses from his youth, said, "Moses, my lord, restrain them." But Moses said to him, "Are you jealous for my sake? Would that all the LORD's people were prophets, that the LORD would put His Spirit upon them!"
>
> Numbers 11:28–29

What was behind Joshua's desire to stop the new prophets? Moses saw that it was jealousy. Joshua, who had been with Moses "from his youth," was threatened by the newcomers. When seventy new prophets were added in a day, all with the same anointing as Moses, Joshua felt his position was jeopardized. His first instinct was to stop them, to get control over the situation.

Moving from prophesying as individuals to prophesying in teams changes a group's dynamic significantly. When newcomers with powerful gifts come into any church or group, their arrival upsets the status quo. People's positions are challenged, and the people who have been there longest are the most vulnerable, because they have the most to lose.

But Moses knew the ways of God. Even hundreds of years before Jesus told the parable of the laborers in the vineyard (see Matthew 20:1–16), Moses understood that God's ways are infinitely higher than the ways of men. Moses responded to Joshua in the same spirit that the owner of the vineyard responded to the laborers who came at the eleventh hour (see Matthew 20:15). Moses loved the generosity of God and did not want Joshua to be jealous. Moses displayed the generous heart of God: He wished everybody could be prophets. He was totally inclusive, not worried about his own reputation. He cared more about the Lord's Spirit being honored and His Kingdom advanced than he cared about having an exclusive place in the Kingdom. Because Moses was "very humble, more than any man who was on the face of the earth" (Numbers 12:3), he was not jealous when new prophets came along. He even rebuked Joshua for his envy and for taking offense.

Frankly, we should expect that God will always bring new prophets along, many of whom will be more gifted than we will ever be. When I was only 27 years old the Lord told me that the greatest thing I would ever do would be to anoint the next generation. It is not the only thing I will do, but in His opinion it is the greatest. Why? Because if we want to be great in God's Kingdom, then we need to be servants of all, even if they are younger, newer and less experienced.

Moses was God's friend (see Exodus 33:11). He knew that his friendship with God could never be altered by who prophesied and who did not, by who had more gifting and who had less. Our relationship with God never comes into question by who does what. Everyone can be God's favorite, and anyone can be His friend if he keeps His commandments (see John 15:14). This is the beautiful thing about the Kingdom of God: It is a Kingdom for "whosoever will"—a Kingdom where everybody can be as close to the King as they want to be.

Different Gifts

But within this same Kingdom, God builds the Body with all kinds of different gifts and talents. To some He gives five talents, to another two, and to another one. The amount of talents that God gives to people is not an indicator of the person's value. The least in the Kingdom is greater than the greatest prophet of the Old Covenant (see Matthew 11:11; Luke 7:28). God is not like people. He does not measure worth by what we do. He measures worth by the fact that we are made in His image. Everyone, therefore, is worth the incalculable cost of the death of His only beloved Son. His friendship with us has never been measured by the gifts He gives us.

In Psalm 27, David prayed an amazing prayer: "One thing have I desired of the LORD . . . that I may dwell in the house of the LORD all the days of my life, to behold the beauty of the LORD" (verse 4, KJV). As a man, David prayed the supreme desire of Jesus' heart, which is echoed in Jesus' prayer in John 17:24, "Father, I desire that they . . . would be with Me where I am to behold My glory." The desires of heaven and earth meet in these two prayers. As we spend time with Him, God gives revelation of Himself so we can draw closer to Him and draw others closer to Him.

In drawing us closer to Him through spiritual gifts, God accomplishes a number of things: He builds His Kingdom, He enables us to help one another, He brings people to conversion and so forth. Every gift from God is given so that we can serve someone else with it.

Serving Others through Prophecy

Although all Christians hear the voice of God for themselves (see John 10:14–16), the gift of prophecy is hearing from God for others. As I shared earlier, prophecy is a gift given to build up the Body of Christ.

> I would like every one of you to speak in tongues, but I would rather have you prophesy. He who prophesies is greater than one who speaks in tongues, unless he interprets, so that the church may be edified.
>
> 1 Corinthians 14:5, NIV

In Paul's study contrasting tongues and prophecy, he underscored the service aspect of prophecy. While the purpose of the gift of tongues is to edify or strengthen one's own spirit, the purpose of the gift of prophecy is to edify or strengthen someone else. Paul makes it clear that it is greater to serve someone else than it is to serve oneself. That is why prophecy is a greater gift than the gift of tongues. And that is why we wish everyone prophesied. We want to have the heart that Moses and Paul had. We want to press in for many to receive and utilize the gift of prophecy, so that the greater Body of Christ will be served and strengthened.

Multiplication

One of the parables by which I live is the parable of the talents. From this Scripture I understand that Jesus wants me to multiply my talent. My heart is moved by this desire because I love to give Him pleasure. What if I could, by impartation and training, raise up hundreds or thousands of prophets, all of whom served His Bride, the Church (see Revelation 21:9)? This is why I position myself to prophesy all the time. I choose to prophesy everywhere I go, whether I feel like it or not. I cannot determine what kind of revelation I will get, but I can determine to serve with my gift in proportion to my faith. I see it as my reasonable service, because God gave it to me in order for it to be multiplied.

For this reason, when the Lord asked me to raise up prophets in my own nation of Canada, I started a national prophetic roundtable. This annual event has now multiplied into high-functioning prophetic roundtables with dozens of prophets in several of the provinces in my nation. Patricia Bootsma, the provincial leader for Ontario, has multiplied everything much more than I. She had relationships with people in Europe, so they came over to Canada to see what we were doing and then went back and started a national roundtable in Holland. And she is currently building relationships to start prophetic roundtables in other nations. The phenomenon just keeps multiplying. All of us work together to hold prophetic conferences, schools, etc., to train up prophets. Across our nation prophets seek to multiply the prophetic anointing as much as God gives us grace. Indeed this is the biblical picture of prophesying in teams.

Prophesying in Teams Brings Fuller Revelation

I love prophesying in teams. It is so easy and enjoyable that I prefer it to prophesying "solo." One reason for this is that no matter who a prophet is, he or she prophesies in part: "For we know in part and we prophesy in part" (1 Corinthians 13:9, NIV). No one person has the full picture. So one of the most beneficial aspects of team ministry is that when we add our pieces of revelation together, we get a much greater understanding of the heart of God in a matter. "Two or three prophets should speak, and the others should weigh carefully what is said" (1 Corinthians 14:29, NIV).

It is sometimes a delicate matter, however, to bring many prophets together, especially when they have differing revelatory gifts. It used to really throw me off when I would be in a group of prophets and my piece of revelation would be different from what others were hearing. I used to doubt myself and think, *Well, maybe I am wrong; maybe I am not hearing correctly.* Or sometimes I would think that other people's pieces were wrong. Both of these are possibilities because nobody is 100 percent accurate all the time (hence the need to judge prophecy). But sometimes it is simply an issue of perspective.

First Corinthians 12 lists several types of revelatory gifts:

> There are different kinds of gifts, but the same Spirit. There are different kinds of service, but the same Lord. There are different kinds of working, but the same God works all of them in all men.
>
> Now to each one the manifestation of the Spirit is given for the common good. To one there is given through the Spirit the message of wisdom, to another the message of knowledge by means of the same Spirit, to another faith by the same Spirit, to another gifts of healing by that one Spirit, to another miraculous powers, to another prophecy, to another distinguishing between spirits, to another speaking in different kinds of tongues, and to still another the interpretation of tongues. All these are the work of one and the same Spirit, and he gives them to each one, just as he determines.
>
> 1 Corinthians 12:4–11, NIV

Revelatory, or prophetic, gifts include "words of wisdom," "words of knowledge," "prophecy," "discerning of spirits," "tongues" and "interpretation of tongues." All six of these gifts fall under the category of revelatory gifts, but all of them function differently.

Solomon had supernatural wisdom, not natural wisdom. He knew by revelation how to solve complex problems (see, for example, 1 Kings 3:16–28). Jesus had a supernatural word of knowledge for the woman at the well regarding her husbands (see John 4). The gift of distinguishing of spirits allows one to sense or see both angels and demons. Tongues are mostly for personal edification (unless they are interpreted), and prophecy is for corporate settings (see 1 Corinthians 14). Each of these revelatory gifts has a different purpose, and therefore, brings a different perspective to a group. I have learned that if I listen carefully when two or three prophets are prophesying differing pieces of revelation, I can actually discern more fully the composite of what the Lord is saying.

An Example of Prophesying in Teams

Let me illustrate with a real life example. The nature of my personal prophetic gift is to see people's destinies and futures. As confirmation of the destiny, the Lord will often give me a specific detail from a person's past. Once our church had some visitors from the United Nations, and one of the women came from a Muslim background. Somehow we got together and they asked for prayer, so I prayed, *Lord, what do You want to say to this person?* Though the woman was not yet a Christian, God began to show me why He had created her. I knew nothing about her, but I could sense her destiny, so I began to prophesy it: "You were created to make wrong things right. You have a special anointing to bring justice, especially to children. The reason you feel this way is because of what happened to you when you were twelve years old . . ." I started to tell her what happened to her when she excitedly cut me off: "Do you know what happened to me when I was twelve years old? Well . . ." And off she went. I did not even get to finish the prophecy because the whole story came tumbling out of her mouth. I then told her that God knew all about her—every detail—and that He wanted her to know Him, too.

A few of us, however, were praying for this non-Christian woman, and one of the prophets had a discernment gift—the prophetic ability to distinguish the source of the spirits working in a person's life (see 1 Corinthians 12:10). This prophet saw an entirely different side to this woman's life. He saw demonic forces at work trying to influence her. He saw wounds and pain that motivated her. He was aghast that I was saying all this good stuff about her when all he could see was danger, danger, danger. It totally shut him down when I prophesied so positively, so he actually said nothing.

Afterward when we talked about it, I said to him, "What you saw was not contradictory to what I saw; it was complementary. I saw her destiny; you saw her struggles. Jesus prophesied both to the churches in the book of Revelation (see Revelation 2 and 3), and He acknowledged both aspects. If you had shared what you saw, then we could have prayed for deliverance and strength in the areas where she struggled so that she would be able to move into the destiny God has for her. The benefit of putting the different perspectives together is that a far more holistic picture is seen, and the Lord can minister to people on a far deeper level."

Appreciating Each Other

Another benefit of prophesying in teams is the appreciation we gain for the whole Body of Christ. When I see others operating in the power of the Holy Spirit, I esteem them more. I think it is beautiful how God chooses and uses such a wide variety of people in unique ways. We learn to honor one another and "esteem one another as better than ourselves":

> Do nothing out of selfish ambition or vain conceit, but in humility consider others better than yourselves. Each of you

should look not only to your own interests, but also to the interests of others.

Philippians 2:3–4, NIV

It took me a long time to learn this lesson. When I first began to prophesy, because I could not see what other prophets saw, I used to assume automatically that their piece was wrong. I would even get mad at others when they brought a different perspective. I did not know how badly I was shutting other prophets down until one day at a reconciliation meeting a woman said to me: "When we prophesy together and I deliver my word, you often say, 'I disagree.' Every time you say, 'I disagree,' I feel like you are saying to me, 'I disregard your word; I don't esteem you; I disrespect you as a person.'" I had to apologize and learn how to hear differing revelation in a new way. I was wrong to disregard other pieces just because they were different. I learned the hard way—after I lost a few relationships. "If I prophesy . . . and have not love, I am nothing." I have been "nothing" more than a few times in my life.

Dave, a native brother in our church, taught me a beautiful lesson on seeing from different perspectives. He was at the home of one of our elders one day when the elder was outside mowing his lawn, trimming his shrubs and pulling weeds. Dave looked at the elder and questioned, "Why do you white guys always do that?"

The elder replied, "Well, I just want it to look better, so I make it all symmetrical."

Dave said, "Do you see that forest across the street? See how none of the weeds are pulled, how there are some high weeds, some low bushes, some short trees and some tall ones? Look at the purple flowers growing right next to the yellow and red ones—all different shapes—no weeds pulled. Now look down the street at all the houses in a row. All the lawns mowed, weeds pulled, etc. Which looks more beautiful?" The elder had to admit that the forest was more beautiful than

201

the manicured lawns. "So why do you white guys always do that?"

We need a new perspective on prophets: Different people with different gift mixes will carry revelation differently. If we learn to work together with all kinds of prophets, then we will naturally grow a spiritual forest instead of a manicured lawn. And the former, when growing and flowing together, will be far more beautiful to everyone who walks through it.

Increased Unity

The final benefit of prophesying in teams is that when we prophesy together we bring about increased unity. And remember that a primary purpose of spiritual gifts is to bring unity:

> It was he who gave some to be apostles, some to be prophets, some to be evangelists, and some to be pastors and teachers . . . until we all reach unity in the faith and in the knowledge of the Son of God and become mature, attaining to the whole measure of the fullness of Christ.
>
> Ephesians 4:11, 13, NIV

Prophecy works with other gifts to bring about unity! Isn't that great? And where there is unity there is blessing (see Psalm 133)!

When we resist prophesying in teams, on the other hand, we can create models that breed division instead. Honoring only one or two prophets in a church breeds a far greater danger of elitism, and this elitism is perpetuated when these prophets isolate themselves from the rest of the Body. It makes it seem like there is an "in crowd" and an "out crowd." This scenario creates jealousy and selfish ambition.

The reality is that every Christian, regardless of gifting, is part of the "in crowd." We are one Body with one Lord, and He gave a multiplicity of gifts to men. When they all work together, His Kingdom is built His way.

Loving God and Others

A well-known prophet tells a story of when he actually died and went to the gates of heaven. He found himself standing in line with a group of people who were about to go into the presence of God. Jesus was standing at the gate welcoming His people. As each person was about to enter heaven, Jesus asked them one question only—the same question: "Did you learn to love?"

If this were the sole question Jesus asked us at the end of our ministries, how would we answer? Jesus Himself boiled the whole "law and the prophets" down to two commandments: Love God and love one another. Prophesying in teams helps us do both.

WHERE IS ECSTATIC PROPHECY HEADED?

14

PROPHETIC, CROSS-CULTURAL EVANGELISM

In case you have not noticed, a spiritual revolution is occurring all over the Western world, particularly in North America. Atheism is out, and almost everything else is in. Everyone is looking for God, but most are not going to a church to find Him. Instead they are visiting psychic shops and psychic fairs, shopping at psychic bookstores, watching psychic television channels and listening to psychic talk shows on the radio. A plethora of New Age variations of spirituality and healing surround us at every turn.

As I have traveled the globe I have found a great hunger for God and for spiritual things. Many times I have read my Bible on an airplane when the person sitting next to me began to ask me questions about God before I even tried to witness to him or her. One time, for example, a man who saw me reading the Bible started telling me the spiritual encounters he had experienced. He shared with me how he and his wife took their newborn babies to psychics to learn what their destinies were. He was excited that the psychic had said his daughter would be gifted in languages and his son in music. He and his wife had taken what the psychic predicted regarding their children so seriously that as soon as their kids were able they enrolled them in language immersion and music classes respectively.

Even at such forums as the UN and the IMF, world leaders have begun to realize the need to factor in spirituality in order to alleviate poverty. They have invited spiritual leaders to their events to teach them how to fuse spirituality and initiatives for the poor.[1] The world indeed has a great hunger for spirituality.

What are Christians to do about this onslaught? Should we just ignore it and hope it will go away? Or should we be sensitive to the fact that unbelievers everywhere are seeking God?

Instead of being fearful of this hunger, Christians should see it as an opportunity to preach the Gospel. We have the answer to modern man's hunger! We have the Holy Spirit living inside us, we have spiritual gifts to demonstrate His reality (see 1 Corinthians 2:4) and we have spiritual words that are packed with power (see 1 Corinthians 2:13; Hebrews 4:12). Perhaps God is setting the world up for radical encounters with the greatest Spirit on the planet: the Holy Spirit! If the Church would understand the opportunity awaiting her, then she could seize this opportunity to introduce searching mankind to the Comforter of all.

Cross-cultural Evangelism

The apostle Paul understood this opportunity when he saw spiritual hunger in the streets of ancient Athens. Acts 17 describes how Paul initially was distressed by all the idolatry he observed (see verse 16). But instead of lambasting the Athenians for their idolatry, he commended them for their hunger, took a cultural cue (the monument to the "Unknown

God") and boldly declared, "What you worship in ignorance, this I proclaim to you" (verse 23). The great apostle Paul was culturally sensitive to the people of Athens. He walked through the city and searched for the felt needs. When he found them, he used them to declare the truth about who God is.

Like Paul, we should take prayer walks through our cities with the sole purpose of trying to identify where our neighbors are spiritually. Perhaps you, too, will be "greatly distressed to see [your] whole city is full of idols" (verse 16). But do not stop at being vexed. Go deeper. Why are there so many idols? What does that tell you? Paul concluded that the people of Athens were "very religious" (verse 22). He did not approach this as a negative thing. Rather, he praised their search for God and then used one of their own idols as a launching pad from which to preach the one true God.

Paul said, "I have become all things to all men, so that I may by all means save some" (1 Corinthians 9:22). A cursory look through the Bible reveals that God spoke to the felt needs of various cultures in order to reach them. That is, He used cultural keys unique to each culture. If it was power that would persuade people, then God moved in power, as He did when Elijah faced the prophets of Baal. If signs were needed, then He gave extraordinary signs, as He did throughout the life of Moses. If it was using a culture's own idol worship, then He used that, as we see in the example of Paul. Obviously God knows how to be seeker sensitive. He knows how to speak the language of a culture in order to reach that culture. Pentecost is the ultimate example of this, with the outpouring of the gift of tongues enabling every nationality to hear the wonderful works of God in their own language. Three thousand got saved that day. The use of cultural keys, therefore, is God's biblical example to preach the Gospel.

The Gentile Church was practically birthed on the streets as obedient men and women went outside the walls of their synagogues and preached the Gospel in homes, in pagan temple courts and on the streets of Roman cities. They took it to the people and taught it in a way that each group would understand. The Gentile Church was birthed with riots, stonings, miracles and signs following the proclamation of their message. It was birthed through an abandoned group of men and women who cared nothing for their own lives or reputations but who were consumed with the desire for Jesus to be known by all. They went to the spiritually needy and demonstrated the truth of their message.

Cross-cultural evangelism proves over and over that this is an effective missions strategy.[2] I have done this myself. I have gone out onto the streets of various cities with the sole purpose of finding out where the average person is spiritually. Sometimes I have written "spirituality surveys" and approached people cold turkey to ask them to fill them out with me. I have learned a lot about where people really are and what they really believe. One of the questions on my survey is "Have you ever had any spiritual encounters? If so, can you please describe them?" It is surprising how many people have either had angelic or demonic encounters. At the end of these surveys I ask people if I can pray for them, and then I ask the Lord for a specific prophecy that will prove He knows them intimately. I have led many people to Christ like this.

Cultural Evangelism in History

Throughout history effective Christians have modeled this biblical principle of cultural evangelism. Hudson Taylor, for example, put on Chinese clothes, wore a long, black braid and culturally became as Chinese as he could in order to win the Chinese people for Jesus. Unfortunately the first people to criticize him were the other missionaries in China who were trying to retain their "Britishness" because they could not differentiate between what was truly Christian and what was merely culture.[3]

Similarly, when Larry Norman used the cultural key of rock music to win a generation being overtaken by it, the first to criticize him were other Christians. His famous song "Why Does the Devil Have All the Good Music?" was inspired by a tract written by the great Reformer Martin Luther, who penned the classic "A Mighty Fortress Is Our God" to a bar tune sung in the taverns of his day. When Larry Norman started, almost no church worship services had drums or electric guitars. Now very few churches do not have them.

Prophetic Evangelism

Of all the evangelism I have ever done—from surveys, to door to door, to street preaching, to church dinners, to friendship evangelism—prophetic evangelism is by far the most effective form of evangelism in which I have engaged. The first time I personally observed its effects was from a man I met in a church in Australia. He told me he had just become a Christian six months ago, and I asked him how that happened. His answer shocked me. "Oh," he said, "I became a Christian at a psychic fair."

I thought I had better explore that a bit, so I said, "Really? Why don't you tell me more about that?"

The man went on to tell me a testimony that forever changed the way I thought about psychics and those who visit them. "I was looking for God," he said, "and I heard that a psychic fair was going to be held in our city."

Inside I was thinking, *If you were looking for God, why did you think He would be at a psychic fair?* Yet the reality is that millions of people flock to psychic fairs, tune in to psychic talk shows and pay money to clairvoyants every day in order to try to touch the supernatural.

So the man decided to go to the psychic fair. Unbeknownst to him, a local church had also heard the psychic fair was coming to town. Instead of praying against it, they decided that the best defense would be a strong offense. Months ahead of time, they began sending intercessors to the place where the fair was to be held to pray for a spiritual breakthrough and for people to be won to Jesus. They also trained up prophetic teams and rented a booth in the middle of the psychic fair. When the time for the fair came, the prophetic teams set up their booth while the intercessors surrounded the facility and prayed nonstop for "a spirit of wisdom and revelation in the knowledge of the one true God" to be revealed right in the midst of the psychic fair. Within a short time, the lines at the booths of the psychics grew smaller and smaller. The psychics began to complain that they were experiencing interference in the spiritual realm, and because of it they had no power. Meanwhile the line at the Christian prophetic booth grew longer and longer, and our man stood in line.

When prophets at the Christian booth prophesied over this man, he began to weep. "They told me so much about my life. They gave me hope and invited me to church. So the next Sunday I went to their church. Within the month, I brought my family. Three months later, our whole family was saved!" Immediately I heard the Spirit of God say to me, 'I want you to do that.' In obedience to that call, I eventually ended up doing prophetic evangelism outreaches in many places.

Since hearing that man's story, I have been involved in numerous prophetic evangelism outreaches. One time I accompanied Patricia King and a number of her prophetic students on an outreach in the streets of Las Vegas. Patricia was planning to produce a program on what people thought about God, so she brought her television team with her. The camera crew was right there as we approached people and began to prophesy over them. I remember one interview vividly. As I prophesied over a man there in the street, speaking God's words of life and healing to him, the man was touched at the core of his being. The "X-treme Prophetic Television" camera zeroed in on the tears welling up in the man's eyes. We discovered later that this man was fresh out of a thirteen-year prison sentence, so he was not a man who cried easily. But there, right out in bold view of everyone on the street with the television crew filming, the ex-prisoner gave his heart to Jesus. One of the last things he said to me was, "I need a mentor!" So we connected him to a pastor in his area. He was only one of the many who became Christians that night as prophets spilled out onto the buses and streets of the needy city of Las Vegas. Reflecting upon the experience, I thought, *The Church is going back to its roots.* That night in Las Vegas reminded me again of the passion of the early Church.

Another significant example in my life of prophetic, cross-cultural evangelism occurred in the city of Stratford, Ontario, last summer. I had visited the city a year earlier and prophesied that God was going to use the Stratford church to reach many homosexuals. Several months later this church led a homosexual to Christ. He was zealous and anxious to bring his friends to God. A year later when I returned to the city to teach at a School of the Prophets, we took a group of students, including this young man, onto the streets and set up a free prophetic booth in front of a coffee shop. It was awesome. Many friends of the young man came for prophecy and prayer because they had seen the radical change in his life. They were prostitutes, transvestites, lesbians, Goths, young people who were living together—all who wanted to know what God had to say about them. Many cried. Others were impressed that God knew them so well, and I was moved with compassion at the brokenness of the lost.

Our cities are full of people just like them, who do not know that God knows them and cares about them. They may be looking for God, but they never darken the door of a church. So we have to seek them out—just like Jesus does.

It is imperative that we prophets understand what God is doing on the earth. He is empowering His Church to reach the lost, and it is not right to keep the gifts God has given us within the four walls of our church buildings.

Ecstatic Prophecy in Evangelism

But what about ecstatic prophecy? What role does it play in the Church's outreach to the lost? The answer may surprise you.

Ecstatic prophecy seems to work with the lost better than it does with the Church. The spiritually hungry are not threatened by the phenomenon of ecstasy; rather, they sometimes are even drawn to it. Their openness to the spiritual realm makes them more comfortable to manifestations such as ecstasy.

I have prayed for dozens of unbelievers, and often I shake, but I always give them a little explanation of what is going on. Often they simply weep, or else they do not seem to care and just listen to the content of what is being said. When they agree with the content they are eager to talk about it, and rarely do they ever bring up or question the manifestations. Sometimes, they even start to tell me their experiences, and we get into some good theological discussions this way.

Give Them What They Need

I challenge you to look around. Everywhere we see that the search for spirituality is a great need in our culture. If our neighbors were poor, we would give them food. If our neighbors were grieving, we would give them comfort. Across North America our neighbors are poor and grieving spiritually. We need to give them what they are searching for. Now is the time to leave our churches and share the spiritual gifts God has given us with our neighbors, our cities, our nations. Be sensitive to the needs around you. And go out into the highways and byways for His sake—so His banquet table will be full.

15

The Coming Global Revival

Prophecy is everywhere. It affects every culture, every religion and every strata of society. In these last days God is preparing the earth for another final supernatural display of His power. Numerous prophets have foretold of a coming end-time revival, and many believe that the greatest revival of mankind is ahead of us. A full-scale global revival is an imminent reality. What we and thousands of others have experienced is about to be replicated en masse throughout the world. And prophecy will play a big part in this worldwide revival.

Bob Jones's Accurate Prophecy

Any serious student of prophecy will find a plethora of words and material from the leading prophetic voices of our age, describing in detail what each one has seen individually. One that bears telling is a prophecy that Bob Jones gave years ago. In August of 1975, Bob was prophesying against abortion. He foresaw the manufacture of a new pill that would have the power to prevent pregnancy even the day after conception. Soon thereafter, a demonic spirit materialized and threatened to kill Bob if he continued to warn people against abortion. Bob rebuked the spirit and kept on prophesying. Within days a large, rock-hard cyst appeared in Bob's stomach. The pain was incredible. The cyst ruptured, and Bob began bleeding internally. Even though Bob knew it was a demonic attack, he was powerless to stop it. He could hardly believe that the devil had that kind of power to take him out. As Bob lay bleeding and dying on his bed, he suddenly felt his spirit leave his body and float upward. Bob kept trying to figure out how a demonic spirit could have done this to him.

The next thing he knew, he was standing in front of the Lord in heaven.[1] Jesus opened His heart wide like two large doors and welcomed believers into heaven. As this was going on, Jesus spoke to Bob and told him to go back and help prepare the Church for a harvest of a billion souls. Though Bob longed to stay in heaven, he willingly acquiesced to the Lord's command. Instantly he found himself back in his body with two angels standing over him prophesying back and forth to one another. One angel asked the other a piercing question: "When will this great harvest take place?" The other angel responded, "This great harvest will begin when the population of the earth reaches six billion."[2]

Ironically, the year when the world's population reached six billion was the year we entered the third millennium: 2000 A.D. For over 25 years Bob proclaimed the coming harvest of a billion souls. In tremendous fulfillment, the decade of the 1990s saw the greatest amount of conversions since the New Testament days of Jesus. Demographers say that within the last fifteen years the Church has witnessed one-third of all conversions since Christ. They have literally poured into the Kingdom.

Biblical Foretelling of the Last Days

The prophets of the Bible also speak of a great end-time harvest (see Romans 11:12–15, 26; Matthew 24:14; Revelation 5:9;

7:9; 14:6; 15:4; Psalm 66:4; Zephaniah 2:11; 3:8–10). While in exile late in his life, the apostle John was allowed to see into the future to the end of time. He recorded in the Apocalypse what he saw:

> After this I looked and there before me was a great multitude that no one could count, from every nation, tribe, people and language, standing before the throne and in front of the Lamb. They were wearing white robes and were holding palm branches in their hands. And they cried out in a loud voice: "Salvation belongs to our God". . . . They fell down on their faces before the throne and worshiped God. . . . Then one of the elders asked me, "These in white robes—who are they, and where did they come from?" I answered, "Sir, you know." And he said, "These are they who have come out of the great tribulation; they have washed their robes and made them white in the blood of the Lamb."
>
> Revelation 7:9–11, 13–14, NIV

This prophecy is both future and global: It foretells that this harvest takes place during the Great Tribulation, and it involves every people group, or *ethnos* (Greek), in the world. John foresaw something of colossal proportions.

Finally, Jesus Himself foretold of this end-time harvest: "This Gospel of the Kingdom will be preached in all the world as a witness to all the nations, and then the end will come" (Matthew 24:14, NKJV). All people groups must be represented; none will be left out.

All Nations Must Hear the Gospel

This has not happened yet. We still have not reached every nation, tribe, people and language. Only recently has it become possible for every people group of the earth to be reached. We are the generation who will see a functioning Church, with at least a portion of the Bible in their own language, existing in every nation, tribe, people and language. What was once far off will be a reality within decades. In fact, Wycliffe Bible Translators projects that between the years 2025 and 2038, Bible translation will have begun in every remaining language community that needs it.[3]

This final success of the missionary movement is accompanied by an exponential increase of Christianity upon the earth. One billion new converts will be added to the current one billion believers. It is not hard to see how, at this rate, the earth will soon contain more saved people than those who are currently in heaven! The Church will see a harvest from every nation.

Recently I attended a historic meeting called "Call2All–Orlando." Mark Anderson, a brilliant missions strategist, led this gathering in Orlando, Florida, which included the CEOs of 170 of the primary missions organizations in the Western world, along with leaders of many international prayer ministries.[4] One of the highlights of this gathering was when the missions and prayer leaders recognized the Lord's hand in establishing them in a strategic alliance to complete God's end-time purpose of bringing the Gospel to every nation on earth. Both movements realized that biblically they were to be one movement, not two (see Luke 10:2; Isaiah 56:6–7; Mark 11:17). These missions leaders divided the earth into 4,000 geographic zones, 6,000 primary languages and 12,000 cultures. Each zone was studied and strategically targeted by the missions movement.

Presently I am involved in a group that participates in prayer and fasting all over the world. This group is a global strategic alliance of international prayer movements that is partnering with the world's missions leaders to reach all 4,000 zones on earth. What this means in a practical sense is that each house of prayer and each intercessor on the earth specifically adopts one missions organization, three individual missionaries and one of the 4,000 zones of the earth to cover in prayer on a regular basis.

I believe this is biblical. God promised that He would establish intercessors who would never be silent until the restoration of Jerusalem:

> I have set watchmen on your walls . . . they shall never hold their peace [keep silent, NASB] day or night . . . and give Him no rest till He establishes . . . Jerusalem a praise in the earth.
>
> Isaiah 62:6–7, NKJV

I further believe Jesus will return in answer to the nations crying out for His leadership (see Revelation 22:17). His coming will be in answer to the mature end-time prayer and worship movement that will operate in great authority (see Luke 18:7–8; Matthew 21:13; Isaiah 62:6–7; 25:9; 27:2–5, 13; 30:18–19; 42:10–13; Joel 2:12–17). The "bowls of prayer" in heaven will be full before Jesus sounds the seven trumpets of judgment upon the earth (see Revelation 8:3). The prayer movement across the globe is now so extensive that in our day we are seeing the reality of the Holy Spirit being joined by the Bride in saying, "Come!"

An Outpouring Accompanied by an Explosion of Gifts

As the prayer movement increases and the missions movement expands, the Holy Spirit is increasingly being poured out upon the earth. And the outpouring of the Holy Spirit is always evidenced by an explosion of spiritual gifts.

Throughout the Bible the "rushing upon" of the Holy Spirit brought about dramatic moves of God. The most noticeable sign at Pentecost was the impartation of spiritual gifts. The disciples spoke in other languages as the Spirit gave them utterance, declaring the wonderful works of God (see Acts 2:11). When Peter stood up to explain the event, he labeled it "the last days outpouring," which had been prophesied by Joel. Peter quoted Joel as he declared:

This is what was spoken by the prophet Joel: " 'In the last days,' God says, 'I will pour out my Spirit on all people. Your sons and daughters will prophesy, your young men will see visions, your old men will dream dreams. Even on my servants, both men and women, I will pour out my Spirit in those days, and they will prophesy. I will show wonders in the heaven above and signs on the earth below, blood and fire and billows of smoke. The sun will be turned to darkness and the moon to blood before the coming of the great and glorious day of the Lord. And everyone who calls on the name of the Lord will be saved.' "

Acts 2:16–21, NIV

For years I believed that Pentecost was primarily about tongues. But having received an ecstatic experience I now realize that a baptism of the Spirit is about receiving an impartation for prophecy, or at least some form of revelatory ability. Acts 2 shows that prophecy, or revelation, is the main evidence of the Spirit being poured out on all people. The interpretation that Peter assigns to the miracle of tongues is prophecy, visions, dreams and prophecy (verses 17–18). Four different expressions of a revelatory nature are given as the primary explanation of the "last days outpouring." Age, gender and maturity are immaterial. The recipients of prophecy, dreams and visions will be young and old, male and female, new and old believers. The Holy Spirit is coming on all flesh.

For Paul, the imparting and releasing of gifts is the manifestation of the Spirit.

Now to each one the manifestation of the Spirit is given for the common good. To one there is given through the Spirit the message of wisdom, to another the message of knowledge by means of the same Spirit, to another faith by the same Spirit, to another gifts of healing by that one Spirit, to another miraculous powers, to another prophecy, to another distinguishing between spirits, to another speaking in different kinds of tongues, and to still another the interpretation of tongues. All these are the work of one and the same Spirit, and he gives them to each one, just as he determines.

1 Corinthians 12:7–11, NIV

"Now to each one the manifestation [*phanerosis*] of the Spirit is given" (verse 7, NIV). The Good News Translation renders it: "The Spirit's presence is shown in some way in each person." It appears that each of the nine gifts is a "showing of the Spirit" in the gathered Church context. Paul is not saying that every single person will receive a manifestation gift, but that to each person to whom one of these gifts is distributed, the Spirit's presence is being made known (continuous present tense). In times of visitation, these nine gifts are especially intensified as they give tangible expressions of the presence or manifestation of the Spirit.

Spiritual gifts are called *pneumatikon* (literally "spirituals"). This word is derived from the Greek, *pneuma*, meaning "spirit" (see 1 Corinthians 12:1; 14:1). Generally speaking, it refers to an expression or embodiment of the Spirit. Spiritual gifts are also called *charismaton* (literally "gifts"), derived from the Greek *charis*, which translates "grace" (see 1 Corinthians 12:4; 1 Timothy 4:14; Romans 12:6). This is where we get the word *charismatic*. This is a more specific term referring to an expression or embodiment of grace. There is a connection between spiritual gifts and God's grace. These manifestations of grace release the gifts, ministries and effects of God's Spirit when He is present in a gathered assembly. The grace, service and effects of the Spirit are His power and presence applied through nine "manifestation gifts." In fact, we could say that all Christians who experience the Spirit are "charismatics." Wherever and whenever the Spirit of God comes, charismatic activity is normal.

Some believe Pentecost was a one-time event, not to be repeated. In some respects this is true. Most would say, however, that the apocalyptic elements of Acts 2:18–20 have still not seen their ultimate fulfillment and therefore still apply to a future generation. Whatever one believes about Pentecost, it is important to realize that the properties of a visitation of the Holy Spirit did not stop with Pentecost. They continue to this day. And it is clear from Scripture that prophecy, dreams, visions and "the rushing upon of the Spirit" (ecstasy) will continue all the way to "the great and glorious day of the Lord" when all who call on His name will be saved (verses 20–21). Prophecy existed pre-Pentecost and will continue until "the perfect comes" (1 Corinthians 13:10). Pentecost did not limit the work of the Spirit but increased it for everyone.

Paul declares, for example, "When you come together, everyone has a hymn, or a word of instruction, a revelation, a tongue or an interpretation. All of these must be done for the strengthening of the church" (1 Corinthians 14:26, NIV). Note the term *revelation*. Note the tongues. When the presence of the Spirit is shown, supernatural revelation is a normal manifestation. It can come through prophecy, words of knowledge, wisdom, mental pictures and so on. In thousands of different settings, I have personally witnessed and heard reports of the operation of every gift listed in 1 Corinthians 12:8–10.

Now in our day, revelation has become a gift for the whole Church (see 1 Corinthians 14:1, 5, 24, 31, 39). Today every person who receives Christ also receives His Spirit, and the Spirit has the ability to impart and release revelation. We can expect in the coming revivals an intensifying of all the gifts—especially prophecy, which in heightened times of the Holy Spirit takes the form of ecstasy.

Empowerment from the Spirit

Another common work of the Holy Spirit during a time of visitation is the empowering of God's people for witness and service. Jesus Himself said, "But you will receive power when the Holy Spirit comes on you; and you will be my witnesses in Jerusalem, and in all Judea and Samaria, and to the ends of the earth" (Acts 1:8, NIV). This is exactly what happened. The Holy Spirit fell, and all the disciples spoke in tongues, looking as though they were drunk, and became witnesses. The effect of this ecstatic demonstration was that thousands were saved on the spot. After the disciples were persecuted by religious leaders who simply could not comprehend this visitation, they went back to the other believers and began to pray. Luke writes, "After they prayed, the place where they were meeting was shaken. And they were all filled with the Holy Spirit and *spoke the word of God boldly*" (Acts 4:31, NIV, emphasis mine). Prophecy and boldness for witness are common fruits of special visitations of God's grace.

Ecstasy: The Catalyst for Mass Salvation

Now here is where ecstatic prophecy and harvest have their connecting point. In Acts 2 we saw the fruit of ecstatic prophecy. We saw that out of the bizarre behavior and the strange tongues came a harvest of three thousand souls in one day—possibly even one hour! Some of those converted on the day of Pentecost would undoubtedly have been those who a mere 53 days earlier were shouting, "Crucify Him! Crucify Him!" As we saw in our Church history discussion (chapter 5), Holy Spirit ecstasy (possession), which often releases revelation in the recipients, is recorded in revival after revival, century after century. A heightened move of the Holy Spirit is almost always connected with the release of ecstatic prophecy. And after this release, these Holy Spirit-possessed firebrands continue to create a movement. Ecstasy, then, is the catalyst for mass salvation. This is why when ecstasy occurs it is so important to discern the source, embrace what is real and lead as many people into the flow of the Holy Spirit as possible.

When ecstasy is real, the manifest presence of God comes down, possessing humans and releasing His testimony. The strange behavior is a secondary aspect, the byproduct of Holy

223

Spirit possession. And ecstasy is almost always followed by ecstatic preaching. Even when ecstasy hits children, they move quickly from revelation (prophecy, dreams and visions) to ecstatic preaching. Prophetic evangelism may bring in converts by the ones and twos, but prophetic ecstasy/ecstatic preaching generally brings in converts by the hundreds and thousands.

In case after case, this is documented. The 1904 Welsh revival began with an ecstatic, Evan Roberts, who incidentally was called "the young prophet." The Brownsville revival was ignited in an ethos of ecstasy and catalyzed by an ecstatic. Azusa Street was full of ecstatics of all forms.

H. A. Baker's *Visions Beyond the Veil* details the progression and the correlation between ecstatic prophecy and mass salvation. This story records an amazing outpouring of ecstatic prophecy and ecstatic preaching among orphaned, beggar children in the Adullam Rescue Mission in China in the 1920s. I record this story as a foreshadowing of things to come.

But from whatever source they came, these children, mostly boys ranging in ages from six to eighteen, had come to us without previous training in morals and without education. Begging is a sort of "gang" system in which stealing is a profitable part. The morals are what would be expected of a "gang" in a godless land. . . . This giving of the Promised Spirit was clearly a love gift of grace "apart from works" or personal merit. It was not something that was worked up. It was something that came down. It was not the result of character building by man from below. It was a blessing of God that came from above. . . .

In the first days of the outpouring of the Spirit one *small boy spoke in pure prophecy* when in the Spirit he seemed to be in heaven at the feet of Jesus. The Lord spoke through him in the first person, clearing up many things the children did not understand and telling them how to tarry and how to seek the Spirit. At that time the Lord said, "When the Spirit is in your midst do not open your eyes, for that will hinder;

the Holy Spirit will descend to give you power to preach the Gospel, to cast out demons and to heal the sick. . . ."

No one present at the time has ever doubted that the Lord spoke to us *by direct inspiration* in the first days of the outpouring of the Spirit when He spoke through one of the smallest and humblest of the children. *There was something about the voice, the penetrating power of those words, a heart-gripping power that cannot be described. We had never heard such a gripping voice from God in any sermon in all our days.* We all knew we were hearing directly from the Lord. Quite a number of the Adullam people later spoke in prophecy. . . .

Many of these visions were given to several at the same time. Nearly all of the visions were seen by quite a number of persons. In many cases the children came to ask if the Bible said anything about certain things they had seen in vision. . . .

After two or three weeks of the Lord's dealing with them, nearly all the children wanted to preach, even the younger ones. There was some real preaching in the power and demonstration of the Holy Spirit. Some of both the younger and older boys hardly seemed like our boys when they preached under the real unction of the Holy Spirit, not timidly and apologetically as before, but as having authority. Hell and heaven, the devil and his power, Christ, His blood, and His salvation, were no myths to these boys. They knew the Lord told them to preach, and they were given the message, "Repent, for the Kingdom of heaven is at hand." As we listened to some of these messages preached with great assurance, warning people to flee from the wrath to come and showing them the wonderful salvation in the love of Christ, our hearts rejoiced within us. When the Power of God was especially great in our midst there was some unusually miraculous preaching.

At the Chinese New Year, when the streets were filled with all classes of people out for a holiday, we Adullam people, having circulated thousands of tracts, formed a circle on the street to preach the Gospel.

One of the older boys had prepared a sermon on a New Year theme. But when the preaching began, the power of God so fell that this boy suddenly began speaking in other tongues, while another person interpreted. One small boy after another preached as interpreter. As soon as the Lord was through with one interpreter he would step back and another feel the unction to preach. As soon as this one stepped into the circle he would get the interpretation. This went on for an hour or two while as many people listened as could get near enough to hear. There were some people of the type that seldom listen to the Gospel who now listened most attentively as these boys spoke with an earnestness that must have seemed strange and unusual. As we came away from that service conducted by the Holy Spirit in such order and beauty, each preacher being of the Lord's appointment, each one speaking the message from Him under direct inspiration, we could but ponder in our hearts at these wonders of God. We seemed to see something of what the preaching of the Church was in the beginning and what it seemed so clear the Lord wanted it to be in the end.

In such preaching the mind of the speaker is entirely inactive, and before utterance he does not know what words the Spirit will speak through his lips. This is pure prophetic preaching. . . .

The Lord was the preacher on several occasions in our little street chapel. For two or three nights the youthful preachers, under the real unction of the Spirit, preached the most inspiring sermons I have ever heard from Chinese evangelists. It seemed as if those sermons would stir anyone to real repentance. God showed His love in still greater power a few nights later. When a boy in his teens was preaching with real power, his eyes suddenly closed and he began to prophesy like an Old Testament prophet under direct inspiration of the Holy Spirit in pure prophecy. The manner of the preacher suddenly changed; the form of the Chinese sentences became rhythmic and perfect; the address changed to the first person, such as, "I am the Lord God Almighty, the one true God, who made all things, who now speaks to you through this boy." "Against me have you sinned." The penetrating words, the sense of having been ushered into the presence of God, I cannot describe. The seats of our little chapel were soon filled, while as many people as could see gathered about the door, listening in awe and wonder.

If there was the least commotion the Lord commanded order, speaking through that boy and saying, "Make no mistake in this matter. Listen carefully and understand. I, the Lord God, have all the authority in heaven and on earth. To Me every man and every demon must give account. I know all about every one of you. I know all your sins. I know how many hairs are on your head. There are 56 of you living in sin here tonight. Repent tonight, and I'll forgive you." For half an hour or more we verily were in the presence of a prophet, as the Lord in this way rebuked those people for idolatry, ungodliness, and all their vices, until there was no ground for hope left anywhere. Then, as in the case of the Old Testament prophets, God spoke of the glories He had prepared for His people. Like a loving Father He pleaded with them to repent that night. He spoke of the coming of distress upon the nations and of the destruction of this ungodly race in the day of God's wrath. All these things were repeated several times with exhortations to listen to every word as from a God who would hold every person present accountable for his own soul after that night.

When the prophecy was finished the boy sat down. There was not a move or a whisper. It seemed to me that every person must know that God was speaking. Nearly all present had come in while the boy's eyes were shut. When the Lord spoke saying there were 56 present bound by the devil and sin, one of the boys carefully counted those not of our own Christian boys. There were just 56.[5]

This short story describes the progression from ecstatic prophecy to ecstatic preaching to revival. As Baptists in 1987, we experienced very similar things. Though we had never heard of ecstatic prophesy, it happened to us almost exactly as the children in Adullam, China. While reading *Visions Beyond the Veil*, I was shocked to discover how similar our experiences were to theirs. Feelings of compulsion and supernatural constraint were common. More often than not our initial prophesying was spoken in imperatives: "You must . . . ," "You must not . . ." "Have I not told you? . . ." A word would be repeated over and over for emphasis. Our early transcripts from twenty years ago contain editorial comments such as "said very loud with much blowing and shaking." In most cases the message would come in first person—as if God Himself were speaking. Sometimes the speaker even would speak to himself in first person as though God were speaking to him. Once, for example, when David Ruis was prophesying he said, "You must do this, too, David!" The presence was so strong that, even years later when I decided to reread those transcripts, both a feeling of nostalgia and nausea swept over me. I almost felt sick to my stomach after being away from these prophetic words for such a long season. When I reread the words, I longed for that time, and I realized how cold we had become and how far we had regressed.

The result of the prophetic ecstasy that occurred in our church was that hundreds were converted to Christ. Non-Christians would come regularly to the services and begin weeping, without knowing what was happening to them. They themselves did not know why they were crying, but they were irresistibly drawn to the love of Christ. Ecstatic prophetic preaching creates revival.

Savanarola: An Ecstatic Preacher

Let me give you another example of ecstatic prophecy producing ecstatic preaching, which in turn produced repentance and revival. Savanarola was an ecstatic, preaching prophet of the late 1400s in Italy. Like Evan Roberts, he was prone to visions and prophetic revelations.[6]

On the evening before he preached his last sermon in Advent, 1492, Savanarola beheld in the middle of the sky a hand holding a sword with the inscription, "Behold, the sword of the Lord will descend suddenly and quickly upon the earth."

Suddenly the sword was turned toward the earth, the sky darkened, and swords, arrows and flames rained down. The heavens quaked with thunder, and the world became a prey to famine and death. The vision ended with a command to the preacher to make these things known.[7]

Savanarola was a prophet, not just a preacher. His prophecies fueled his preaching and caused men to turn to God wherever he went. He was bold, fearless and utterly unintimidated. He could not be bought or sold by those with wealth or power and prophesied repeatedly against worldliness. This "mad" monk set all of Florence into a swoon—including the wealthy Medici family and artists Michelangelo, DaVinci and Boticelli. In his dying days, the brilliant ruler of the Florentine state, Lorenzo, called Savanarola to his bedside. Even though they were enemies in life, Lorenzo summoned Savanarola in death because, he said, "I know of no honest friar save this one." Savanarola's message to him was again of repentance. Soon after Savanarola was martyred for his bold stand. True prophets lead men back to God.

Ecstatic Prophecy in Finland

In the 1800s the nation of Finland saw the remarkable phenomenon of ecstatic preaching prophets, who came to be known as the "Finnish trance preachers." One of the most renowned among them was a nine-year-old girl named Karolina Utriainen (b. 1843). God used a trance, which lasted almost a whole day, to call this girl to preach His Word.

Karolina described her experience as a dream, but it was a typical ecstatic vision. She looked into heaven, her eyes were blinded by the glory, and she fell to the ground. In the vision she saw Christ Himself, who showed her a book and commanded her to preach. She described her vision as follows: "The Lamb came to me, lifted me up and said, 'Fear not, little friend; as I have chosen you to carry out my commands, I have by this vision wished to confirm my words to you.' Then He gave me a great book written with golden letters and ordered me to preach the Gospel of peace. And then I awakened out of my dream."[8]

From this point on Karolina became a prophetic revivalist with frequent attacks of ecstasy and preaching fits. An eyewitness describes the awesome sense of dread that accompanied her:

> A chill crept over her limbs, and small red dots appeared on her skin. Her heart began to throb violently, and she felt a tingling sensation in her arms. A morbid glitter was seen in her eyes, and her face became pale. A weak shiver and giddiness attacked her. Everything darkened, and suddenly the preacher threw herself backwards. She moistened the fingers of her right hand with her lips and made the hand a great arc just as if she were turning a page in a very large book. Then with a terribly distended chest, and in a voice loud enough to fill a medium-sized church, she began to speak. Her legs were always stiff and inflexible, and the skin apparently senseless and dripping in sweat. Once the attack was over, she wakened without any conspicuous symptoms, beyond the fact that she had completely forgotten what she had said during the trance. Of the visionary elements which presented themselves at the very outset there persisted only a faint recollection.[9]

It was said that Karolina caused a tremendous sensation, and many were of the opinion that the end of this world was approaching.

Follow the Lamb

The nations are waiting to be harvested, and how we live and what we believe matters. A universal, global move of the Spirit of God has been promised, and it will come.

The correlation between ecstatic prophecy/preaching and the salvation of large portions of the surrounding population has been proven throughout the centuries—from the Book of Acts onward. Ecstatic prophecy in history reveals an underlying theme: God loves the world, but the world does not yet love Him. In order to solve the dilemma, God comes close. He hides Himself from the wise and prudent and reveals Himself to babes. Not the wise and noble of this world (see 1 Corinthians 1:26), but those who become like little children recognize His presence. Though they may not understand the foolishness of God (see 1 Corinthians 1:25), people can be drawn forcefully into His Kingdom through ecstasy. Either they or others they observe become possessed by the Holy Spirit, and they have revelations of God.

It is my firm conviction that ecstatic prophetic revival preaching will be one of the manifestations of the last days. It has been the way God has spoken through His prophets from the beginning, and it will continue until the end. Let us, then, "follow the Lamb wherever He goes" (Revelation 14:4).

Notes

Introduction

1. Hans Urs von Balthasar, *Prayer*, trans. Graham Harrison (San Francisco: Ignatius Press, 1986), 164–65.

Chapter 2 The Universality of Ecstatic Prophecy

1. Evelyn Underhill, *Mystics of the Church* (Cambridge: James Clarke & Co., 1925; American ed., Harrisburg, Penn.: Morehouse Publishing, 1988), 29.

2. J. Lindblom, *Prophecy in Ancient Israel* (Minneapolis: Fortress Press, 1962), 27.

3. Ibid., 29. Emphasis mine.

4. Ira Friedlander, *The Whirling Dervishes* (New York: Macmillan, 1975), jacket flap.

5. http://houseofturkey.org/drupal/node/17 (accessed December 10, 2007).

Chapter 3 Ecstatic Prophecy is Biblical

1. Clarke Garrett, *Origins of the Shakers* (Baltimore: Johns Hopkins University Press, 1987), 7.

2. From personal correspondence with Dr. Daniel Juster, March 11, 2008.

3. Henry M. Morris, *The Genesis Report* (Grand Rapids: Baker Books, 1976), 52.

4. J. Lindblom was professor of exegetical theology in Lund from 1930 to 1947. His research into Old Testament prophecy had been conducted over a period of nearly forty years before he wrote his classic, *Prophecy in Ancient Israel*. He is considered one of the foremost scholars in the study of the Old Testament prophets.

5. David Aune is currently professor of the department of theology at Notre Dame University and holds the following degrees: B.A., Wheaton College; M.A.,

233

Wheaton Graduate School of Theology; M.A., University of Minnesota; Ph.D., University of Chicago. Professor Aune specializes in the study of the New Testament in the context of Greco-Roman society and culture. He is currently at work on a commentary on the Testament of Solomon for De Gruyter and a book on Greco-Roman culture and the New Testament for the Anchor Bible Reference Library, as well as a book on early Christian worship with Professor Maxwell Johnson. Aune has written or edited 15 books and has written 85 articles and 100 book reviews. He was awarded a Fulbright visiting professorship at the University of Trondheim, Norway (1982–83) and an Alexander von Humboldt Research Prize at the University of Tübingen, Germany (1994–95), was inducted into the Norwegian Royal Academy (Det Kongelige Norske Videnskabers Selskab) in 2001, and was the Annual Professor at the Albright Institute for Archaeological Research in Jerusalem, Israel (2002–2003). He has also written the biblical commentaries, "Revelation 1–5," *Word Biblical Commentary*, vol. 52a (Waco: Word Books, 1997); "Revelation 6–16," *Word Biblical Commentary*, vol. 52b (Waco: Word Books, 1998); and "Revelation 17–22," *Word Biblical Commentary*, vol. 52c (Waco: Word Books, 1998). See some of his work in the following reviews: Robert P. Seesengood, *Restoration Quarterly* 41 (1999), 59–60; Giancarlo Biguzzi, *Biblica* 79 (1998), 582–85; and Christopher Rowland, *Journal of Theological Studies* 50 (1999), 735–38.

6. Dr. Robinson held the following degrees: Litt. D. (Camb), D.D. (Lond), Hon. D.D. (Aberdeen), Hon. D.Th. (Halle).

7. T. H. Robinson, *Prophecy and the Prophets in Ancient Israel* (New York: Charles Scribner's Sons, 1923), 31.

8. Ibid., 40.

9. Lindblom, *Prophecy*, 47. Emphasis mine.

10. Ewald, Haevernick and Bleek agree (see Samuel Davidson, *Introduction to the Old Testament*, vol. 2 [Edinburgh: Williams and Norgate, 1862], 230), as does also Gustav Friedrich Oehler (*Old Testament Theology* [Chicago: University of Chicago Press, 1904], 363).

11. R. Laird Harris, Gleason L. Archer Jr. and Bruce K. Waltke, *Theological Wordbook of the Old Testament* (Chicago: Moody, 1980), 544.

12. Robert Jamieson, A. R. Fausset and David Brown, *Introduction to the Prophetical Books/Jamieson-Fausset-Brown Bible Commentary* (Epiphany Software, electronic text and markup, 1999). Emphasis mine.

13. Francis Brown, S. R. Driver and Charles A. Briggs, *The Brown-Driver-Briggs Hebrew and English Lexicon* (1907; repr., Peabody, Mass.: Hendrickson Publishers, 1996), 610, 612. Emphasis mine.

14. Charles D. Isbell, "The Origins of Prophetic Frenzy and Ecstatic Utterance in the Old Testament World," http://209.85.173.104/search?q=cache:xpJj SqwQauEJ:wesley.nnu.edu/wesleyan_theology/theojrnl/11-15/11-5.htm+ (accessed February 12, 2008).

15. Ibid. Emphasis mine.

16. David Aune, *Prophecy in Early Christianity and the Mediterranean World* (Grand Rapids: Eerdmans, 1983), 86.

17. John White, *When the Spirit Comes in Power* (Westmont, Ill.: InterVarsity Press, 1989), 25.

18. Lindblom, *Prophecy*, 48.

19. Aune, *Prophecy in Early Christianity*, 33.

20. Lindblom, *Prophecy*, 4–5.

21. Aune, *Prophecy in Early Christianity*, 86.

22. Robinson, *Prophecy and the Prophets*, 31.

23. James Strong, *Strong's Talking Greek & Hebrew Dictionary, Englishman-Strong's Concordance* (Winterbourne, Ont.: Online Bible, 1993), Greek #1611. Emphasis mine.

24. Spiros Zodhiates, *The Complete Wordstudy Dictionary: New Testament* (Chattanooga: AMG Publishers, 1992), s.v. "Ekstasis." Emphasis mine.

25. W. E. Vine, *Vine's Expository Dictionary of Old and New Testament Words* (Grand Rapids: Revell, 1981), s.v. "trance" (*ekstasis*).

Chapter 4 Biblical Ecstasy and the Consciousness of the Prophet

1. Isbell, "Origins." Emphasis mine.

2. See Abraham J. Heschel, *The Prophets*, vol. 2 (New York: Harper & Row, 1975). See chapter 9, "The Theory of Ecstasy," and chapter 10, "An Examination of the Theory of Ecstasy," for a detailed synopsis of both Jewish and Christian views on biblical ecstasy.

3. Ibid., 134.

4. Ibid., 134–36.

5. Ibid., 137–46.

6. "Let the Fire Fall" Conference at the Anaheim Vineyard (Anaheim, California), July 1994.

7. Although I was shaking wildly while prophesying, I was aware of what was happening both within and without and could stop it.

8. Henry Baird, *The Huguenots* (New York: Charles Scribner, 1895), 186–87.

9. Plato lived 427–348 B.C. The Septuagint was written in the mid-third century B.C. (285–247).

10. Lindblom, *Prophecy*, 28.

11. Ibid.

12. Ibid.

13. Ibid.

14. Thomas W. Gillespie, *The First Theologians: A Study in Early Christian Prophecy* (Grand Rapids: Eerdmans, 1994), 157. Emphasis mine.

15. Gordon D. Fee, *The New International Commentary on the New Testament: The First Epistle to the Corinthians* (Grand Rapids: Eerdmans, 1987), 685.

16. Alex MaCalister, *The International Standard Bible Encyclopedia*, ed. James Orr (Peabody, Mass: Hendrickson Publishers, 1994), s.v. "trance." Emphasis mine.

Chapter 5 Ecstasy—The Ways of God and the Mind of Man

1. Cecil M. Robeck Jr., *Prophecy in Carthage: Perpetua, Tertullian and Cyprian* (Cleveland: The Pilgrim Press, 1992), 203; Aune, *Prophecy in Early Christianity*, 20–21; Lindblom, *Prophecy*, 179; Garrett, *Origins*, 6.

2. Aune, *Prophecy in Early Christianity*, 86–87.

3. Ibid.

4. Even when prophesying out of the gift, I want to underscore my understanding that the information comes from God. The information is not in me but comes as a gift that He gives, only by His favor; as such, I can always receive from Him at some level.

5. Aune, *Prophecy in Early Christianity*, 86.

6. The Russian scientist Ivan Pavlov, a Nobel Peace Prize laureate, did a series of experiments with dogs that revealed there were conditional reflexes to external stimuli. For example, Pavlov recorded that the conditioned response of drooling occurred when external stimuli were given at the same time as the dogs were given food.

7. Abraham J. Heschel, *The Prophets* (Peabody, Mass.: Prince Press, 1962), 26. Emphasis mine.

Chapter 6 Can Ecstasy Be Controlled or Induced?

1. Heschel, *Prophets*, 86–87.

2. Ibid., 87.

3. Lindblom, *Prophecy*, 59–60.

Chapter 7 Ecstatic Prophecy in Church History

1. John White, *When the Spirit Comes with Power: Signs and Wonders Among God's People* (Downers Grove, Ill.: InterVarsity Press, 1988).

2. Aug Poulain, *The Catholic Encyclopedia*, vol. 5, transcribed by Marcia L. Bellafiore (New York: Robert Appleton Company, 1909). Emphasis and additions mine.

3. Aune, *Prophecy in Early Christianity*, 313. Emphasis mine.

4. Ibid. Emphasis mine.

5. http://www.tertullian.org/readfirst.htm#22 (accessed January 2, 2008).

6. Tertullian, *Early Christian Writings, The Passion of the Holy Martyrs Perpetua and Felicitas*, http://www.earlychristianwritings.com/text/tertullian24.html (accessed January 6, 2008). Emphasis mine.

7. David Yount, "Why Did Quakers Stop Quaking?" *Quaker Life News*, March 2002, http://www.fum.org/QL/issues/0203/why_did_quakers.htm (accessed March 3, 2008).

8. George Fox, *The Journal of George Fox*, ed. Rufus M. Jones (Richmond: Friends United Press, 1908; repr. 1976), 215–16.

9. David S. Lovejoy, *Religious Enthusiasm in the New World: Heresy to Revolution* (Cambridge, Mass.: Harvard University Press, 1985), 124.

10. Bradford Keeney, *Shaking Medicine: The Healing Power of Ecstatic Movement* (Rochester, Vt.: Destiny Books, 2007).

11. François-Maximilien Misson, *Le Théâtre Sacré des Cévennes. Ou Récit de diverses merveilles nouvellement opérées dans cette Partie de la Province du Languedoc* (London: Roger Robert, 1707; repr. Paris: Les Éditions Paris, 1996). 205.

12. Abbott Brueys, *A History of Fanaticism in Our Time* (Paris: Muguet, Francois, 1692), as quoted in *The Prophetic Movement in the Cévennes or The Anointing of the Holy Spirit on France: Reflections on the Prophetic Movement in the Cévennes*

in the 17th and 18th Centuries, M. Henning Schikora Mas David, F 30360 Vézénobres, France; email: Cevennes@hotmail.com.

13. Patrick Dixon, *Signs of Revival* (East Sussex, UK: Kingsway Publications, 1994), 122.

14. Ibid.

15. Ibid., September 8, 1784.

16. Ibid., July 29, 1759.

17. Ibid.

18. Ibid., August 5, 1784.

19. Richard F. Lovelace, *Dynamics of Spiritual Life* (Westmont, Ill.: InterVarsity Press, 1980).

20. Jonathan Edwards, *Jonathan Edwards on Revival* (Carlisle, Penn.: Banner of Truth, 1965), 151–54.

21. "Spiritual Awakenings in North America," *Christian History* vol. 8, no. 3, issue 23 (Summer 1989), 26.

22. Winkey Pratney, *Revival* (Springdale, Penn.: Whitaker House, 1984), 125–26.

23. Keith J. Hardman, *The Spiritual Awakeners* (Chicago: Moody Press, 1983), 145–46.

24. "Charles Grandison Finney," *Christian History* vol. 7, no. 4, issue 20 (Fall 1988), 2–3.

25. Richard M. Riss, "The Manifestations throughout History," paper presented at Catch the Fire Conference, St. Louis, Mo., 1995.

26. Ibid.

27. Frank Bartleman, *Azusa Street* (St. Paul: Logos, 1980), 59–60.

Chapter 8 Discerning the Spiritual Source

1. Nancy Caciola, *Discerning Spirits: Divine and Demonic Possession in the Middle Ages* (Ithaca, N.Y.: Sage House, 2004).

2. According to the *Encarta World English Dictionary* (New York: St. Martin's Press, 1999), a level is a "calibrated glass tube containing liquid with an air bubble in it, mounted in a frame and used for measuring whether surfaces are horizontal. Also called spirit level."

3. Robeck, *Prophecy in Carthage*, 9.

4. J. B. Lightfoot and J. R. Harmer, *The Apostolic Fathers*, 2nd ed., ed. Michael W. Holmes (Grand Rapids: Baker Books, 1989), 189.

5. Ibid., 230.

Chapter 11 Prophesy According to Faith

1. Kenneth Stevenson, *Law, Liberty, and the Pursuit of Godliness* (Nashville: Xulon Press, 2002), 77.

2. Smith Wigglesworth, *Ever Increasing Faith*, ed. Adam Woeger (Springfield, Mo.: Gospel Publishing House, 1924). Also printed in "The Discerning of Spirits," *The Pentecostal Evangel*, December 8, 1923.

3. See www.beahero.org.

Chapter 14 Prophetic, Cross-cultural Evangelism

1. Peter Gardener, *Praying at the Global Gates* (Llanelli, UK: self-published, 2004), 19.

2. For further study on this topic, I recommend *Eternity in Their Hearts* by Don Richardson (Ventura, Calif.: Regal Books, 1981).

3. Hudson Taylor of China, http://www.newcovenantfellowship.us/Outreach_ Ministries/russian_missions.html (accessed March 23, 2008). Also check out the websites of the following prophetic ministers: Rick Joyner, Cindy Jacobs (http:// www.generals.org/index.php?id=1654), Mike Bickle (www.ihop.org), Bob Jones and Kim Clement.

Chapter 15 The Coming Global Revival

1. To hear the full story, listen to *"Open Heavens Vol. 1: Supernatural Experiences of the Prophets Today,"* with Bob Jones, Todd Bentley, Stacey Campbell and Lou Engle. A.R.M.M.E. Resources Inc., 2003 (CD available from www.revivalnow .com).

2. Ibid.

3. See http://www.wycliffebibletranslators.com/about/Progress/tabid/463/ Default.aspx.

4. See www.call2all.org.

5. H. A. Baker, *Visions Beyond the Veil* (New Kensington, Penn.: Whitaker House, 1973; repr. 2006). Emphasis mine.

6. Philip Schaff, *History of the Christian Church*, vol. 6: *The Middle Ages*, ed. David S. Schaff (Grand Rapids: Eerdmans, 1910; repr., New York: Charles Scribner's Sons, 1991), 688.

7. Ibid., 694.

8. Lindblom, *Prophecy*, 14–15.

9. Ibid.

Selected Bibliography

Aune, David E. *Prophecy in Early Christianity and the Ancient Mediterranean World.* Grand Rapids: Eerdmans, 1983. The most profitable resource I have found on the prophetic. The notes and subject index are especially helpful.

———. "Revelation." *Word Biblical Commentary,* vol. 52. General editors David A. Hubbard and Glen W. Barker; New Testament editor Ralph P. Martin. Dallas: Word Books, 1997.

Avila, St. Teresa of. *The Life of Teresa of Jesus.* Translated by E. Allison Peers. New York: Image Books, 1991. The primary resource on St. Teresa's ecstatic phenomena. Apparently her Mother Superior demanded she explain thoroughly what was happening to her. This book was the result.

Baird, Henry. *The Huguenots.* New York: Charles Scribner, 1895. Helpful for a historical basis.

Bickle, Mike. *Growing in the Prophetic.* Lake Mary, Fla.: Charisma House, 2008. A good overview from the viewpoint of the early Kansas City years.

Bouyer, Louis, Jean Leclercq and Francoi Vandenbroucke. *A History of Christian Spirituality,* vols. 1–3. New York: The Seabury Press, 1982. Fantastic, probably one of the most definitive Catholic sources on spirituality. It is possible to breeze through to the place that meets your fancy and then find enough of an overview to send you on the path to further research.

Brown, Francis, S. R. Driver and Charles A. Briggs. *A Hebrew and English Lexicon of the Old Testament (Based on the Lexicon of William Gesenius as Translated by Edward Robinson)*. Gloucestershire, UK: Clarendon Press, 1974.

Burgess, Stanley M. *The Spirit and the Church: Antiquity*. Peabody, Mass.: Hendrickson Publishers, 1894. A good source of original quotes from the early Church Fathers (100–500 A.D.) concerning the Holy Spirit.

Cairns, Earle. *An Endless Line of Splendor*. Carol Stream, Ill.: Tyndale, 1986. Excellent source, tracing the major revivals of the last 250 years.

Chevreau, Guy. *Praying with Fire*. London: Marshall Pickering, 1995. Contains historical material about St. Teresa of Avila.

DeArteaga, William. *Quenching the Spirit*. Lake Mary, Fla.: Creation House, 1992.

Deen, Edith. *Great Women of the Christian Faith*. Uhrichsville, Ohio: Barbour & Co. Inc., 1959. Loaded with a hundred cameo biographies of great Christian women, it is helpful to scan for visionaries, to understand the broad strokes of their lives.

Deere, Jack. *Surprised by the Power of the Spirit*. Grand Rapids: Zondervan, 1993. What can we say? The best!

Dixon, Dr. Patrick. *Signs of Revival*. East Sussex, UK: Kingsway Publications, 1994. Good on the current renewal/revival. Especially helpful on the English context and historical stuff.

Edwards, Jonathan. *A Treatise on Religious Affections*. Grand Rapids: Baker, 1982.

———. *Edwards on Revival*. London: Banner of Truth Trust, 1965.

———. *The Works of Jonathan Edwards*. 2 vols. London: Banner of Truth Trust, 1992.

Faussett, A. R. "Introduction to the Prophetical Books." In Jamieson, Fausset and Brown's *Commentary on the Whole Bible*. Grand Rapids: Zondervan, 1999.

Fee, Gordon D. "The First Epistle to the Corinthians." *The New International Commentary on the New Testament*. Grand Rapids: Eerdmans, 1987. A huge section on 1 Corinthians 12–14.

Garrett, Clark. *Origins of the Shakers*. Baltimore: Johns Hopkins University Press, 1987.

Gillespie, Thomas W. *The First Theologians: A Study in Early Christian Prophecy*. Grand Rapids: Eerdmans, 1994.

Greig, Gary S. and Kevin N. Springer, eds. *The Kingdom and the Power*. Ventura, Calif.: Regal Books, 1993. General Kingdom essays.

Heschel, Abraham J. *The Prophets*. Peabody, Mass.: Prince Press, 1962.

Isbell, Charles D. "The Origins of Prophetic Frenzy and Ecstatic Utterance in the Old Testament World." http://209.85.173.104/search ?q=cache:xpJjSqwQauEJ:wesley.nnu.edu/wesleyan_theology/ theojrnl/11-15/11-5.html (accessed February 12, 2008).

Jones, Brynmor Pierce. *An Instrument of Revival: The Complete Life of Robert Evans*. Alachua, Fla.: Bridge-Logos Publishers, 1995. A must-buy concerning Evan Roberts of the Welsh revival of 1904, with really good little peeks into his personal life and struggles.

Laird, Harris, L. Gleason and R. Archer Jr. *Theological Wordbook of the Old Testament*. Chicago: Moody, 1980.

Lewis, I. M. *Religion in Context: Cults and Charisma*. Cambridge: Cambridge University Press, 1986.

Lightfoot, J. B. and J. R. Harmer. *The Apostolic Fathers*. 2nd ed. Edited by Michael W. Holmes. Grand Rapids: Baker, 1989.

Lindblom, J. *Prophecy in Ancient Israel*. Philadelphia: Fortress Press, 1973. One of the best books ever written on the cultural contexts of the ancient Israelite prophets, and the standard work quoted by most other authors on the subject.

Lovejoy, David S. *Religious Enthusiasm in the New World*. Cambridge, Mass.: Harvard University Press, 1985. A scholarly critique that contains interesting material others may never have heard of.

MaCalister, Alex. "Trance." *International Standard Bible Encyclopedia*. General editor James Orr, Peabody, Mass.: Hendrickson Publishers, 1994.

Poloma, Margaret. *By Their Fruits: A Sociological Assessment of the Toronto Blessing*. Toronto: TACF Publishing, 1994.

Poulain, Aug. *The Catholic Encyclopedia*, vol. 5. Transcribed by Marcia L. Bellafiore. New York: Robert Appleton Company, 1909.

Pytches, David. *Prophecy in the Local Church*. London: Hodder & Stoughton, 1993. A helpful overview.

Orr, J. Edwin. *The Flaming Tongue*. Chicago: Moody, 1973. Excellent, especially on the Welsh revival.

Riss, Richard. *A Survey of 20th Century Revival Movements in North America*. Peabody, Mass.: Hendrickson Publishers, 1988.

Robeck, Cecil M. Jr. *Prophecy in Carthage*. Cleveland, Ohio: The Pilgrim Press, 1992. The first of its type to come out, and without equal. It exegetes some prophecies and visions from the early Church in North Africa. Especially helpful on Montanism, Tertullian and ecstatic prophecy of the third century A.D.

Robinson, T. H. *Prophecy and the Prophets in Ancient Israel*. 2nd ed. London: Gerald Duckworth and Co. Ltd., 1953.

Schaff, Philip. *History of the Christian Church*. 8 vols. Grand Rapids: Eerdmans, 1910. A place to dig around in the era of your choice.

Stronstad, Roger. *The Charismatic Theology of St. Luke*. Peabody, Mass.: Hendrickson Publishers, 1984. Very good.

Tucker, Ruth A. and Walter L. Liefeld. *Daughters of the Church*. Grand Rapids: Zondervan, 1987. Ruth writes with a bit of flair, revealing warts and all. Reminiscent of Edith Deen's book *Great Women of the Christian Faith*. There is a helpful section on religious women of medieval times.

Underhill, Evelyn. *Mystics of the Church*. Cambridge, Mass.: James Clarke & Co., 1925. Reprint, Harrisburg, Penn.: Morehouse Publishing, 1988.

Von Balthasar, Hans Urs. *Prayer*. Translated by Graham Harrison. San Francisco: Ignatius Press, 1986.

Williams, Don. *Revival: The Real Thing*. La Jolla, Calif.: Coast Vineyard, 1995.

SCRIPTURE INDEX

243

245

Subject Index

Stacey Campbell has a passion to teach believers, through sound teaching and strong values, to know how to hear the voice of God, and she speaks with a prophetic voice to this generation. She is the founder and facilitator of the Canadian Prophetic Council and serves as an honorary member of the Apostolic Council of Prophetic Elders. Stacey has been ordained and is much sought after as an international conference speaker, ministering in more than sixty nations.

Stacey and her husband, Wesley, have also founded a global mercy organization, Be a Hero (www.beahero.org), working in 27 nations to care for children at risk. The Campbells founded and pastored a church in Kelowna, British Columbia, for twenty years. Presently they serve Kelowna Christian Centre as part of the apostolic team. The prayer, prophetic and revival dimension of their ministry is called Revival NOW Ministries (www.revivalnow.com).

Producers of the ten-CD *Praying the Bible Series*, they also have co-authored two books, *Praying the Bible: The Pathway to Spirituality* and *Praying the Bible: The Book of Prayers*. They are members of the teaching faculty of the Wagner Leadership Institute and are the international directors for The Call.

Wesley and Stacey live in Kelowna, B.C., with their five children. Contact Stacey at:

P.O. Box 25077
Mission Park, Kelowna BC V1W 3Y7
Canada
(250) 717-1003
websites: www.heroresources.com
www.revivalnow.com
e-mail: Stacey@revivalnow.com

Praying the Bible Series

The *Praying the Bible Series* is a collection of ten CDs featuring powerful prayers using Scripture set to inspired musical accompaniment. Interspersed with intercession and prophecy, the dramatic, fervent prayers will transport you into the throne room of heaven. Praying along with these CDs will enrich your own times of devotion and intercession and teach you the age-old practice of personal, audible Bible prayer.

Open Heavens, Vols. 1 and 2

In *Open Heavens, Vols. 1 and 2*, Stacey Campbell, Lou Engle, Bob Jones and Todd Bentley relate supernatural experiences—visions, stories and encounters with God and His angels. Set to enthralling music, you will be encouraged and uplifted and gain a broader understanding of God's spirit realm.

Praying the Bible: The Pathway to Spirituality

Praying the Bible: The Pathway to Spirituality is a concise presentation of the oldest model of prayer spanning over two thousand years. Learn the importance of prayer and how to go about it—and why God's Word is the one and only source of true prayer power. Everyone who engages in this proven method of prayer will experience a marked improvement in his or her prayer life.

Praying the Bible: The Book of Prayers

By Jesus' example, we know that praying the Scriptures aloud produces powerful results. *Praying the Bible: The Book of Prayers* presents complete passages of Scripture in distinct prayer sections. A unique and long-overdue prayer tool for novice pray-ers, seasoned intercessors and everyone who seeks more consistent, sustained prayer and a deeper life with God.